CHRIST'S VICTORIOUS KINGDOM

Postmillennialism Reconsidered

John Jefferson Davis

AUDUBON PRESS
2601 Audubon Drive / P.O. Box 8055
Laurel, MS 39441-8000   USA

Orders: 800-405-3788
Inquiries: 601-649-8572
Voice: 601-649-8570 / Fax: 601-649-8571
E-mail: buybooks@audubonpress.com
Web Page: www.audubonpress.com

Cover design by Crisp Graphics

ISBN # 0-9742365-3-5

Preface to the 2006 Audubon Press Edition

I am grateful to the editor and staff of Audubon Press for bringing my book *Christ's Victorious Kingdom: Postmillennialism Reconsidered* back into print. I still believe that the biblical, theological, and historical arguments presented in the original edition of 1986 are still valid, and help to recover for today's church a hopeful view of the advance of Christ's kingdom that was widely held by earlier generations of Puritan and Reformed scholars, and which helped to energize the modern missionary movement.

This current year of 2006, twenty years after the first appearance of the book, also would seem to be an appropriate and auspicious time for its republication, in that this year marks both the two hundredth anniversary of the Haystack prayer meeting at Williams College that sparked the birth of the American missionary movement, and the one hundredth year anniversary of the Azusa Street revival in Los Angeles that marked the birth of the modern Pentecostal movement.

In the two decades since the original publication of *Christ's Victorious Kingdom,* the global church has continued to grow in a remarkable way in Asia, Africa, Latin America, and other parts of the world. It is my hope that a new generation of readers may find in this book new inspiration and vision for participating in the work of the resurrected, reigning, and returning Lord of the Church as he extends his kingdom in the world through the work of missions, evangelism, and the preaching of the gospel.

John Jefferson Davis   July, 2006
Hamilton, Massachusetts

Contents

Preface to the 1986 Baker Book House Edition

Several years ago, in the course of giving lectures on biblical eschatology, I was struck by the fact that postmillennialism, now almost totally forgotten in conservative circles, was for much of the nineteenth century the dominant millennial understanding. The fact that godly and learned conservative scholars, such as John Owen, Jonathan Edwards, Charles Hodge, Robert L. Dabney, and Benjamin B. Warfield held this view suggested that there must be some biblical underpinnings for this perspective that were worth reexamining. Is there in fact a biblical basis for the expectation of unprecedented revival in the church prior to the return of Christ at the end of the age?

A second factor that sparked my interest in this older eschatological perspective is the mounting evidence of the remarkable growth of the Christian church in Latin America, Africa, Korea, China, and other parts of Asia. The "mustard seed" of Christ's kingdom is evidently displaying dramatic growth before our very eyes.

It is to be acknowledged from the outset that it is difficult or perhaps impossible for any one eschatological framework to integrate all the diverse and complex data of the Old and New Testaments in this area. Nevertheless, it is argued that the merits of the postmillennial framework deserve a fresh consideration in today's church. It is my hope in particular that readers who are directly involved in the missionary and evangelistic outreach of the church may gain fresh encouragement for their labors from the biblical vision of the victorious, reigning Christ at the right hand of the Father–the vision that is central in this work.

I wish to express my appreciation for the comments and criticisms made by my students, colleagues, and friends during the various stages of this project. A special word of thanks is due to Patrick Henry and other colleagues at the Institute for Ecumenical and Cultural Research in Collegeville, Minnesota, where much of this research and writing was done. The limitations and shortcomings, however, remain my own.

John Jefferson Davis   1986
Hamilton, Massachusetts

cult or perhaps impossible for any one eschatological framework to integrate all the diverse and complex data of the Old and New Testaments in this area. Nevertheless, it is argued that the merits of the postmillennial framework deserve a fresh consideration in today's church. It is my hope in particular that readers who are directly involved in the missionary and evangelistic outreach of the church may gain fresh encouragement for their labors from the biblical vision of the victorious, reigning Christ at the right hand of the Father—the vision that is central in this work.

I wish to express my appreciation for the comments and criticisms made by my students, colleagues, and friends during the various stages of this project. A special word of thanks is due to Patrick Henry and other colleagues at the Institute for Ecumenical and Cultural Research in Collegeville, Minnesota, where much of this research and writing was done. The limitations and shortcomings, however, remain my own.

John Jefferson Davis
Gordon-Conwell Theological Seminary
South Hamilton, Massachusetts
1986

1

Introduction

Does the Bible teach that conditions in the world will become steadily worse as history unfolds and the time of Christ's return draws nearer? Are Christians destined to minority status, marginal influence in society, and inevitable defeat prior to the second coming? Or does the Bible teach that there will be a remarkable period of peace, spiritual prosperity, and victorious expansion for the church prior to the return of Christ at the end of the age?

Both understandings of biblical eschatology have, at different times in church history, been widely held among Bible-believing Christians. These eschatological questions are not merely idle speculation about date-setting, but presuppose a philosophy of history and an understanding of the lordship of Christ that have practical and pervasive implications for the believer's involvement in missionary outreach, evangelism, and social renewal.

The present work is an attempt to present a fresh exam-

ination of the more optimistic of the eschatological out-
looks mentioned, the position which has come to be known
as postmillennialism. This view, not widely held in twentieth-century America, and now largely forgotten, was in
fact the dominant view among Bible-believing Christians
in this country during the last century. It will be necessary
to clearly define the term *postmillennialism*, clear up
some common misunderstandings concerning this position, examine its biblical basis, consider important objec-
tions to it, and explore its implications for missionary
activity and social reform.

The point of view presupposed in the present work is
that biblical eschatology is fundamentally a matter not of
calendar but of Christology. Developing an eschatological
understanding is not a matter of assembling isolated texts
in some artificial scheme, but rather one of gaining a comprehensive and integrated perspective of the sovereign
God's purposes for human history. The New Testament's
witness to the ongoing activity of the victorious, resurrected Christ, now exalted to a place of universal authority
at the right hand of the Father, extending his kingdom
through his Word and Spirit, provides the central focus in
relation to which other relevant passages of Scripture are
to be understood.

What Is Postmillennialism?

The main tenets of the postmillennial position as it was
generally held during the nineteenth century can be out-
lined as follows:

1. Through the preaching of the gospel and dramatic outpourings of the Holy Spirit Christian missions and
   evangelism will attain remarkable success, and the

church will enjoy an unprecedented period of numerical expansion and spiritual vitality.

2. This period of spiritual prosperity, the millennium, understood as a long period of time, is to be characterized by conditions of increasing peace and economic well-being in the world as a result of the growing influence of Christian truth.
3. The millennium will also be characterized by the conversion of large numbers of ethnic Jews to the Christian faith (Rom. 11:25–26).
4. At the end of the millennial period there will be a brief period of apostasy and sharp conflict between Christian and evil forces (Rev. 20:7–10).
5. Finally and simultaneously there will occur the visible return of Christ, the resurrection of the righteous and the wicked, the final judgment, and the revelation of the new heavens and the new earth.[1]

This perspective is called postmillennial because in this understanding Christ will return after the period of millennial blessing, not prior to it, as is taught in various forms of the premillennial view.[2] While in the postmillennial view Christ is not physically present on earth during the millennial period, he is the active agent and primary cause of the church's victorious advance and expansion, sending forth the Spirit to bless in a dramatic way the proclamation of the Word of God. (The word *millennium* is derived from the Latin *mille* [thousand] and refers to the thousand-year period spoken of in Revelation 20:4–6.)

---

1. Clarence Augustine Beckwith, "The Millennium," *The New Schaff-Herzog Encyclopedia of Religious Knowledge,* ed. Samuel Macauley Jackson, 13 vols. (New York: Funk and Wagnalls, 1910), vol. 7, p. 377.

2. For good introductions to the various millennial positions, see Robert G. Clouse, ed., *The Meaning of the Millennium: Four Views* (Downers Grove: InterVarsity, 1977), and Millard J. Erickson, *Contemporary Options in Eschatology: A Study of the Millennium* (Grand Rapids: Baker, 1977).

Some Misunderstandings
About Postmillennialism

Since postmillennialism is a position which has not been widely held in recent times, some contemporary authors in their references to it have not given an accurate representation of its true nature and claims. Several common misunderstandings call for comment at this point.

In the first place, the postmillennial perspective is not to be confused with nineteenth-century "evolutionary optimism" or some secular notion of progress. This eschatological view came to prominence among Puritan churchmen in seventeenth-century England long before the Darwinian theory of evolution made its impact in the Western world. According to the postmillennial outlook, any amelioration of social evils is not the result of immanent forces at work within history, nor primarily of merely human effort, but essentially is the result of the supernatural influence of the ascended Christ through his Word and Spirit, working through his people. A spiritually revitalized church is understood to have an increasingly positive impact on the surrounding world and its structures through its preaching, social ministry, and the example of its own inner life.

In the second place, postmillennialism is not to be identified with liberalism or the "social gospel." As will be shown, this eschatological perspective arose within an orthodox theological context, and in nineteenth-century America was espoused by notable conservative theologians such as Charles Hodge, A. A. Hodge, Robert L. Dabney, W. G. T. Shedd, A. H. Strong, and Benjamin B. Warfield.

The postmillennial vision of the spreading kingdom of Christ not only energized the great nineteenth-century efforts in home and foreign missions, but also from 1815 onward motivated social reforms in the areas of peace, temperance, public education, the abolition of slavery, and concern for the poor.[3] There was a widespread conviction during this period that the advancing kingdom of Christ required not only personal regeneration but also efforts to redeem and transform unrighteous social structures.

As the nineteenth century wore on, however, many of the theological underpinnings of the original postmillennial outlook were eroded in the more liberal wings of American Protestantism. An early "social gospeller" such as Washington Gladden (1836–1918) still insisted on personal regeneration as a fundamental precondition for lasting social change, but with later leaders in the social-gospel movement such as Josiah Strong (1847–1916) this classic evangelical tenet receded in importance. As historian Jean B. Quandt has observed, with Strong "Christ . . . the giver of grace and the lord of history became Christ the teacher and example. Conversion was replaced by moral effort."[4]

For Lyman Abbott (1835–1922), a Congregational minister and leader in the social-gospel movement, the kingdom of God would come through immanent historical forces and institutions: schools, science, legislation, the press, and the churches. The kingdom that was to be ushered in by fresh outpourings of the Holy Spirit was, in the later, secularized versions of postmillennialism in the social-gospel movement, replaced by advances in knowledge, culture, and ethical Christianity.[5] This secularized form of postmillennialism represented in the social-gospel movement has caused some later observers to confuse this eschatological outlook with theological liberalism. The

---

3. Timothy L. Smith, "Righteousness and Hope: Christian Holiness and the Millennial Vision in America, 1800–1900," *American Quarterly* 31:1 (1979): 21. See also *Revivalism and Social Reform in Mid-Nineteenth-Century America* (Nashville: Abingdon, 1957) by the same author, especially chapters 5, 10, and 14.

4. Jean B. Quandt, "Religion and Social Thought: The Secularization of Postmillennialism," *American Quarterly* 25 (1973): 396.

5. Ibid., pp. 396, 399.

historical record shows, however, that while classic postmillennialism and the social gospel shared a vision for
social transformation, their theological presuppositions
concerning the nature of sin and salvation were quite different. Historic postmillennialism should not be tarred
with the brush of a later theological movement which attempted to reproduce its social fruits without maintaining
its original doctrinal roots.

In the third place, postmillennialism is not to be confused with universalism, the doctrine that all will ultimately be saved. The postmillennial perspective looks
toward a future period of history when the number of those
truly converted to the Christian faith will be very great,
but at no time does it expect that all will be converted or
that sin will be entirely eliminated prior to the eternal
state. Postmillennialists do expect a time prior to the return of Christ when a revitalized Christianity will become
the world's dominant religion and most powerful moral
and intellectual influence, but this is not to be equated
with any expectation of universal salvation.

In the fourth place, the postmillennial outlook should
not be identified with some version of "manifest destiny"
which sees the United States as the key to God's plan for
enlarging his kingdom in the world. This confusion has,
unfortunately, occurred in the past. In the nineteenth century Hollis Read, a Congregational minister and missionary to India, believed that God's millennial purposes were
being fulfilled in America. In his two-volume work, *The
Hand of God in History*, Read attempted to show that
geography, politics, learning, the arts, and morality all
pointed to the coming of the millennium in America.
From this base the millennial blessings could spread
throughout the earth. The extension of Anglo-Saxon
culture and political control over other nations could facil-
itate the spread of the gospel.[6]

---

6. Cited by Robert G. Clouse, "Millennium, Views of the," *Evangelical
Dictionary of Theology*, ed. Walter A. Elwell (Grand Rapids: Baker, 1984),
p. 717.

Although God may choose to use a particular nation at some juncture of history in a very strategic way, his saving purposes are not bound to any political state or institution, whether the United States or any other society. American Christians have contributed in a very significant way to the cause of world missions, and are obligated to continue to do so in light of their abundant financial, educational, and organizational resources. If American Christians fail to rise to the continuing and growing challenges of world evangelization, God will certainly raise up other churches to accomplish his will. The dramatic increase in missionary interest and activity in Third-World churches is seen by some as evidence that this is in fact already beginning to take place.

It should be understood that the postmillennial perspective provides a forecast for the global and long-term prospects of Christianity, but not for the local, short-term prospects of denominations or churches in the nation. Postmillennialists expect that during the special period of millennial blessing the church as a whole will be revitalized, but it is not expected that the pathway in time to that point will exhibit uniform progress on all fronts for all visible churches and denominations. The advance of the kingdom of God against the kingdom of darkness can be thought of as the spiritual equivalent of a world war. The tide of the war as a whole may clearly be running in one direction rather than the other, but this does not mean that the victorious side does not experience setbacks and temporary defeats on various fronts on the way to ultimate victory.

In other words, the merits of the argument for the postmillennial perspective are not to be tied to the judgments about the present or near-term prospects of the Christian church in America. God could send a great revival to the United States, or he could send catastrophic judgment: which will in fact prove to be the case is known infallibly only to God. The point to be underscored is that postmillennialism offers a global, long-term perspective about the future of the church and not short-term local predictions for particular churches and nations.

Voices from the Past

Since postmillennialism is such an unfamiliar position to most Christians in America today, it is worthwhile to recall the conservative biblical scholars and theologians of earlier generations who were committed to this understanding of the Scriptures. John Calvin, one of the greatest leaders of the Protestant Reformation, had an understanding of the kingship of Christ that paved the way for the full flowering of the postmillennial view in English Puritanism. In the 1536 preface to the *Institutes of the Christian Religion,* addressed to Francis I, king of France, Calvin expressed his confidence in the triumph of the Reformation faith, empowered as it is by Christ the King:

> But our doctrine must tower unvanquished above all the glory and above all the might of the world, for it is not of us, but of the living God and his Christ whom the Father has appointed King to "rule from sea to sea, and from the rivers even to the ends of the earth" (Ps. 72:8; 72:7, Vg.). And he is so to rule as to smite the whole earth with its iron and brazen strength, with its gold and silver brilliance, shattering it with the rod of his mouth as an earthen vessel, just as the prophets have prophesied concerning the magnificence of his reign (Dan. 2:32–35; Isa. 11:4; Ps. 2:9, conflated).[7]

Calvin's confidence in the spread of Christ's kingdom is also expressed in his commentaries and sermons. God will show "not only in one corner, what true religion is . . . but

---

7. John Calvin, *Institutes of the Christian Religion,* ed. John T. McNeill, trans. Ford Lewis Battles, 2 vols. (Philadelphia: Westminister, 1960), vol. 1, p. 12. The Scripture references in parentheses have been added by the editor.

. . . will send forth His voice to the extreme limits of the earth."[8] Countless offspring "who shall be spread over the whole earth" shall be born to Christ.[9] The Holy Spirit was given to the church in order to "reach all the ends and extremities of the world."[10] Calvin's outlook does not, of course, represent a fully articulated postmillennialism, but it does foreshadow subsequent developments.

It is generally stated that postmillennialism came into prominence through the writings of the Anglican commentator Daniel Whitby (1638–1726), but prior to the publication of Whitby's widely read *Paraphrase and Commentary on the New Testament* in 1703, this outlook was being articulated by Puritan scholars such as Thomas Brightman, William Gouge, John Cotton, and John Owen.[11] On October 24, 1651, Owen preached a sermon before the House of Commons on the theme of "The Kingdom of Christ" in which his postmillenarian outlook is quite evident. That God in his appointed time would "bring forth the Kingdom of the Lord Christ unto more glory and power than in former days, I presume you are persuaded," he stated to the assembly. He believed that the Scriptures foretold a time in history of "multitudes of converts, many persons, yea nations, Isa[iah] 60:7.8, 66:8, 49:18–22; Rev[elation] 7:9," and "professed subjection of the nations throughout the whole world unto the Lord Christ, Dan[iel] 2:44, 7:26, 27, Isa[iah] 60:6–9."[12] Owen, who at the time was dean of Christ Church College, Oxford, is frequently considered to be the most able English biblical scholar of his generation.

The Savoy Declaration of 1658, which adapted the West-

8. Commentary on Mic. 4:3.
9. Commentary on Ps. 110:3.
10. Sermon on Acts 2:1–4.
11. Peter Toon, ed., *Puritans, the Millennium and the Future of Israel: Puritan Eschatology 1600 to 1660* (Cambridge: James Clarke, 1970), p. 6.
12. William H. Goold, ed., *The Works of John Owen*, 16 vols. (1850; London: Banner of Truth, 1967), vol. 7, p. 334.

minster Confession of Faith to the needs of the Congregational churches in England, incorporated a postmillennial statement:

> according to his promise, we expect that in the latter days, Antichrist being destroyed, the Jews called, and the adversaries of the kingdom of his dear Son broken, the churches of Christ being enlarged and edified through a free and plentiful communication of light and grace, shall enjoy in this world a more quiet, peaceable, and glorious condition than they have enjoyed. [26.5]

The Savoy Declaration was adopted by the American Congregational churches in the Synod of Boston, 1680, and in the Synod of Saybrook, Connecticut, in 1708,[13] prior to the beginning of the Great Awadening in 1720. The date of its adoption is an indication that the convictions expressed were not merely an optimistic reflection of revival in the churches, for such revival was yet future for the congregations of New England.

It is well known that Jonathan Edwards, considered by many to be the greatest theologian that America has ever produced, held to the postmillennial outlook. In the context of the Great Awakening, Edwards in his 1747 treatise, "An Humble Attempt to Promote Explicit Agreement and Visible Union of God's People in Extraordinary Prayer," encouraged his fellow ministers to engage in united, sustained concerts of prayer to promote revival consistent with the coming of Christ's kingdom. The main fulfillment "of those prophecies, that speak of the glorious advancement of Christ's kingdom on earth, is still to come," he wrote. There were good reasons to hope that "that work of God's Spirit will begin in a little time, which in the progress of it will overthrow the Kingdom of Antichrist, and

---

13. Philip Schaff, ed., *The Creeds of Christendom*, 6th ed., 3 vols. (reprint ed.; Grand Rapids: Baker, 1983), vol. 3, p. 723.

in its issue destroy Satan's visible kingdom on earth."[14] The progress of the Great Awakening in New England led Edwards to believe that the latter-day glory of the church spoken of in the prophets could be drawing near.

The postmillennial hope represented by Edwards did not die in America with the passing of the Great Awakening; it was strongly represented, for example, in the nineteenth-century Princetonian tradition of Archibald Alexander, J. A. Alexander, and the Hodges.[15] In his *Systematic Theology* Charles Hodge wrote that the "common doctrine of the Church . . . is that the conversion of the world, the restoration of the Jews, and the destruction of Antichrist are to *precede* the second coming of Christ, which event will be attended by the general resurrection of the dead, the final judgement, the end of the world, and the consummation of the Church."[16]

What Hodge termed the "common doctrine of the Church" was at least the dominant view in the nineteenth century. In 1859 the influential theological quarterly, the *American Theological Review,* could assert without fear of contradiction that postmillenialism was the "commonly received doctrine" among American Protestants.[17] Theologians in the South such as Dabney and James Henley Thornwell, Shedd of Union Seminary in New York, the Baptist theologian A. H. Strong, and Patrick Fairbairn in Scotland were all of this persuasion.[18]

14. *The Works of Jonathan Edwards,* vol. 5, Stephen J. Stein, ed., *Apocalyptic Writings* (New Haven: Yale University Press, 1977), pp. 335, 412. This volume also contains Edwards's postmillennial interpretation of the Book of Revelation.

15. See Greg Bahnsen, "The Prima Facie Acceptability of Postmillennialism," *Journal of Christian Reconstruction* 3:2 (1976–77): 48–105, for a good survey of this position in church history.

16. Charles Hodge, *Systematic Theology,* 3 vols. (1872–73; Grand Rapids: Eerdmans, 1968), p. 861. Italics added.

17. Cited by James H. Moorhead, "The Erosion of Postmillennialism in American Religious Thought, 1865–1925," *Church History* 53:1 (1984): 61.

18. See Bahnsen, "The Prima Facie Acceptability of Postmillennialism." Fairbairn's views are expressed in *The Interpretation of Prophecy* (1856; London: Banner of Truth, 1964), especially pp. 442–93.

The postmillennial perspective of Old Princeton was continued in the work of Warfield, who was professor of theology at Princeton from 1887 to 1921. In an article on "The Prophecies of St. Paul," Warfield gives special attention to 1 Corinthians 15:20–28 and its statements about the resurrected Christ and his continuing conquests in history:

> It is immediately seen to open to us the nature of the whole dispensation in which we are living, and which stretches from the First to the Second Advent, as a period of advancing conquest on the part of Christ. During its course He is to conquer "every rulership and every authority and power" (verse 24), and "to place all His enemies under His feet" (verse 25), and it ends when His conquests complete themselves by the subjugation of the "last enemy," death. We purposely say, period of "conquest," rather than of "conflict," for the essence of Paul's representation is not that Christ is striving against evil, but progressively (ἔσ-χατος, verse 26) overcoming evil, throughout this period.[19]

According to Warfield, 1 Corinthians 15:20–28 depicts the risen Christ as engaged in a victorious campaign of warfare against all spiritual opposition, a campaign in which only death itself—the "last enemy"—remains to be defeated at the second advent and general resurrection, understood as coterminous events. Conservative Christians in this century have relied heavily on Warfield's masterful defenses of biblical inspiration, but have generally overlooked this aspect of his exegesis and eschatology.

By the end of the First World War the postmillennial position was in eclipse, with premillennial and amillennial views gaining the ascendancy. The pessimism and disillusionment engendered by wartime conditions con-

---

19. Benjamin B. Warfield, *Biblical and Theological Studies,* ed. Samuel G. Craig (Philadelphia: Presbyterian and Reformed, 1952), p. 485. The essay originally appeared in 1886.

tributed heavily to the demise of the once-dominant view in American Christianity. The optimistic and hopeful outlook of the postmillennial vision no longer seemed suited to the times. It has, however, been maintained by a few conservative writers in this century such as Loraine Boettner and J. Marcellus Kik,[20] and also by R. J. Rushdoony, Greg Bahnsen, Gary North, and David Chilton.[21]

In a recent article Stanley N. Gundry argued the intriguing thesis that changes in the dominant eschatological positions over the course of church history had as much to do with the changing social climate as with purely exegetical considerations. Gundry suggested that optimistic periods of history favored postmillenial orientations, while premillennialism gained in favor during periods of historical turbulence and pessimism.[22] Could it be that while premillennialists and postmillennialists have read the same Bible, one group has focused on the shadows and the other on the light? In any case, it is a rather notable fact that an impressive body of conservative, orthodox Bible scholars—Owen, Edwards, the Hodges, Strong, Shedd, Fairbairn, and Warfield, among others—was convinced by study of the Scriptures that the

---

20. Loraine Boettner, *The Millennium* (Philadelphia: Presbyterian and Reformed, 1957); J. Marcellus Kik, *An Eschatology of Victory* (Nutley, N.J.: Presbyterian and Reformed, 1971).

21. Rushdoony and his followers are exponents of the so-called theonomic outlook, which argues for the abiding validity and applicability of the criminal sanctions of the Mosaic law. It should be noted that while these "theonomists" are postmillennialists, not all postmillennialists are theonomists: the two positions are logically distinct. Owen, for example, in a 1652 sermon on "Christ's Kingdom and the Magistrate's Power," clearly distinguished the moral and civil components of the Mosaic legislation in terms of their contemporary applicability, holding that only the moral component is "everlastingly binding." *The Works of John Owen*, vol. 8, p. 394. David Chilton's *Paradise Restored* (Tyler, Tex.: American Bureau for Economic Research, 1984) is an exposition of Revelation from a postmillennial standpoint.

22. Stanley N. Gundry, "Hermeneutics or *Zeitgeist* as the Determining Factor in the History of Eschatologies?" *Journal of the Evangelical Theological Society* 20:1 (1977): 45–55.

church is to make dramatic progress in the world prior to the coming of Christ. What is the biblical basis for such a hope? It is to an examination of specific Old and New Testament texts that we now turn.

2

The Witness
of the Old Testament

"Christianity . . . shall not only overcome all opposition, but overtop all competition; it shall be exalted above the hills." This comment on Isaiah 2:2 by Matthew Henry was typical of the optimistic outlook of earlier generations of evangelical biblical scholars. What other strands of Old Testament thought led such godly and learned students of Scripture to maintain such a hopeful outlook on the prospects for the advance of the Christian faith in the world? As we shall see, there is indeed a biblical basis for the vision of the advancing, victorious kingdom of Jesus Christ, foretold in the Old Testament and then more fully revealed and actually inaugurated in the New Testament. The two main foci of this chapter will be the Abrahamic covenant, in which God reveals his universal saving purpose, and the messianic promises and prophecies which reveal the means by which the divine purpose is to be realized in history.

The Abrahamic Covenant

"I will bless those who bless you, and him who curses you I will curse; and by you all the families of the earth shall bless themselves" (Gen. 12:3). In this first revelation of the Abrahamic covenant, God reveals his desire to bring blessings not only upon Abraham and his family, but ultimately upon "all the families of the earth." At times in her history the nation of Israel relapsed into a very narrow and parochial understanding of her role in God's redemptive plan, but from the beginning it was not so. The God of Abraham clearly intended to bring salvation not only to Israel, but through this people, to all the peoples of the earth.

It is difficult to overestimate the strategic role of the Abrahamic covenant in the design of God's redemptive plan. The noted conservative scholars of the last century, K. F. Keil and Franz Delitzsch, rightly note that this text (Gen. 12:3) condenses "the whole fulness of the divine counsel for the salvation of men into the call of Abram."[1] All further redemptive promises were in fact only expansions and closer definitions of that promise of salvation held out to the human race in that first declaration.[2] As the Jewish scholar Umberto Cassuto has pointed out, inherent in the promise of Genesis 12:3 is the concept of the global reach of God's salvation, a theme which would be subsequently developed in the teaching of the prophets.[3]

The term used in 12:3, *mispachah* (families), denotes a circle of relatives, a social unit related by blood, marriage, or adoption. By extension the term can be used of a tribe or

---

1. K. F. Keil and Franz Delitzsch, *Biblical Commentary on the Old Testament* (25 vols.), *The Pentateuch*, trans. James Martin, 3 vols. (Grand Rapids: Eerdmans, 1949), vol. 1, p. 193.

2. Ibid., p. 194.

3. Umberto Cassuto, *A Commentary on the Book of Genesis*, trans. Israel Abrahams, 2 vols. (Jerusalem: Magnes Press, 1964), vol. 2, p. 315.

a people, as in Amos 3:2, of Israel as a nation: "You only have I known of all the families of the earth."

It is worth noting that the first statement of the salvation covenant speaks in terms of families rather than isolated individuals or nation-states. The heavenly Father, "from whom every family in heaven and on earth is named" (Eph. 3:15), desires that the family structure, so basic to human society and yet now so marked by the effects of sin, should be a primary sphere for the revelation of the redeeming action of his grace. This family emphasis, so prominent in the Scriptures, has not always been adequately recognized in evangelical understanding of the plan of salvation.

After Lot and Abraham separate, following strife between their herdsmen and Abraham's gracious offer of the choice of land to his nephew, God confirms his earlier promise to the patriarch. "I will make your descendants as the dust *(aphar)* of the earth; so that if one can count the dust of the earth, your descendants also can be counted" (Gen. 13:16). The term used for "dust" here is quite common in the Old Testament, as in Genesis 2:7, "the LORD God formed man of dust from the ground." Elsewhere it is also used figuratively to suggest a very great number, as in Numbers 23:10, where Balaam asks, "Who can count the dust of Jacob, or number the fourth part of Israel?" Even if allowance is made for Semitic hyperbole in such usage, it is clear that God is promising to Abraham an immense progeny, a line and number of descendants that far surpasses any natural human expectation. As Gerhard von Rad has stated, this promise of innumerable descendants is "a primary ingredient in the promise to the patriarchs."[4]

After the account of the war with the kings recounted in chapter 14, and the rescue of Lot, God again speaks to

---

4. Gerhard von Rad, *Genesis: A Commentary,* trans. John H. Marks (Philadelphia: Westminster, 1961), p. 160.

Abraham, who is concerned that he is yet childless. It seems that God's promises are not being fulfilled. The Lord brings Abraham outside at night and says, "Look toward heaven, and number the stars, if you are able to number them." Then God says, "So shall your descendants be." Abraham believes God, and that faith is "reckoned . . . to him as righteousness" (Gen. 15:5, 6). Abraham is promised descendants as numberless as the stars of heaven. Abraham's faith is demonstrated in his willingness to put more stock in the unconditional promises of God than in his own human assessment of the visible progress of God's purpose in the world. This is a healthy reminder and example for present-day students of biblical eschatology. The promises of God in Scripture, and not present world conditions, should be the decisive factor in our hope for the future prospects of the people of God in history.

When Abraham is ninety-nine years old, God appears to him yet another time to confirm his saving purposes: "I will make you exceedingly fruitful; and I will make nations of you, and kings shall come forth from you" (Gen. 17:6). To reinforce the promise, God changes his name from Abram (exalted father) to Abraham (father of a multitude). The repetition of the promise of countless progeny underscores the importance in God's intention of this aspect of the Abahamic covenant.

The climactic test of the patriarch's faith is recounted in chapter 22, where God calls on Abraham to sacrifice Isaac, his beloved son and heir of the promise. It seemed that God himself was dashing the means by which the promise of many descendants would be fulfilled. But Abraham, not wavering in faith, obeyed God, considering that God is able to raise men even from the dead (Heb. 11:19; see also Rom. 4:20–21). Abraham's heroic obedience was rewarded with yet another emphatic confirmation of the covenant: "I will indeed bless you, and I will multiply your descendants as the stars of heaven and as the sand which is on the seashore. And your descendants shall possess the gate of their enemies, and by your descendants shall all the nations of the earth bless themselves, because you have obeyed my voice" (Gen. 22:17–18). Earlier references to descendants as numerous as the stars of heaven and the sand of the seashore are here combined. The faith of Abraham is to be a means of bringing spiritual blessings to all the nations of the earth.

The statement that Abraham's descendants shall "possess the gate of their enemies" is the promise of spiritual and cultural dominance of the godly covenant people. John Calvin comments on this phrase, noting that the text means that "the offspring of Abraham shall be victorious over their enemies; for in the gates were their bulwarks, and in them they administered judgement."[5]

After the death of Abraham, the covenant is confirmed to Isaac, in language reminiscent of the earlier promises: "I will multiply your descendants as the stars of heaven, . . . and by your descendants all the nations of the earth shall bless themselves: because Abraham obeyed my voice and kept my charge, my commandments, my statutes, and my laws" (Gen. 26:4–5). Similarly, God confirms his covenant with Jacob, demonstrating the continuing validity of the promise to Abraham: "I am the LORD, the God of Abraham your father and the God of Isaac; . . . your descendants shall be like the dust of the earth, . . . and by you and your descendants shall all the families of the earth bless themselves" (Gen. 28:13–14).

From the perspective of New Testament revelation, it becomes clear that the Abrahamic covenant is fulfilled through Jesus Christ, God's Messiah and instrument of salvation to the world. It was God's design that "in Christ Jesus the blessing of Abraham might come upon the Gentiles" (Gal. 3:14). Those who have faith in Jesus Christ are indeed Abraham's offspring, heirs according to the prom-

---

5. John Calvin, *Commentaries on the First Book of Moses, Called Genesis*, trans. John King, 2 vols. (Grand Rapids: Eerdmans, 1948), vol. 1, pp. 572–73.

ise (Gal. 3:29; cf. Acts 3:25–26). It is through the Christian
church and the gospel of Jesus Christ that God will bring
into the world a body of believers as countless as the stars
of heaven and the dust of the earth. The New Testament
Great Commission (Matt. 28:19–20) to disciple all nations
is in fact founded on the Abrahamic covenant's revelation
of God's will to bring spiritual blessing to all nations. It is
God's design in the Great Commission not merely that all
nations receive a "witness" of the gospel, but that a countless multitude actually be brought to living faith in the
one true God, in fulfillment of the Abrahamic covenant.
This covenant is not superseded in the New Testament
but, as Paul clearly teaches, provides the essential foundation for the inclusion of the Gentiles in God's saving
purpose. The resurrected Christ, himself the great missionary and apostle, stands behind the Great Commission,
and through his power and might the promises to Abraham will surely be fulfilled.

The Messiah and His Kingdom

The instrumentality of the Messiah in fulfilling God's
redemptive purposes is foreshadowed in the messianic
promises and prophecies of the Old Testament. In the
Psalms we find clear pictures of a great king, God's Messiah, ruling over a vast kingdom that far transcends the
boundaries of the nation Israel.

The Messianic Psalms

Psalm 2, which may have for its historical background
some rebellion of a surrounding nation against David or
an Israelite king of the Davidic line, has to be read in the
light of the New Testament:

> "I have set my king
>   on Zion, my holy hill."

> I will tell of the decree of the LORD:
> He said to me, "You are my son,
>   today I have begotten you.

Ask of me, and I will make the nations your heritage,
and the ends of the earth your possession.
You shall break them with a rod of iron,
and dash them in pieces like a potter's vessel." [vv. 6–9]

Verse 7, "You are my son, today I have begotten you," is quoted by the apostle Paul in Acts 13:33 in an evangelistic sermon in the synagogue at Pisidian Antioch: "what God promised to the fathers, this he has fulfilled to us their children *by raising Jesus;* as also it is written in the second psalm, 'Thou art my Son, today I have begotten thee'" (italics added). According to Paul, Psalm 2:7 has been fulfilled in the resurrection of Jesus. Jesus Christ, the son of David, is now enthroned in the heavenly Zion by virtue of his resurrection from the dead and ascension to the right hand of God. By virtue of his death and resurrection, he has rightful authority over the nations, and has only to ask the Father that they be given to him as his heritage (v. 8). As Keil and Delitzsch point out, Jehovah "has appointed the dominion of the world to His Son: on His part therefore it needs only the desire for it, to appropriate to Himself that which is allotted to Him."[6]

And does the resurrected Christ desire that the nations be made his heritage? The answer is emphatically in the affirmative, as may be seen in Christ's command to the disciples in the Great Commission: "All authority in heaven and on earth has been given to me. Go therefore and make disciples of all nations . . ." (Matt. 28:18–19).[7] The Father's offer to make the nations the Son's possession is realized through the Great Commission, as the church in obedience preaches the gospel and Christ sends forth

---

6. Keil and Delitzsch, *Biblical Commentary, The Psalms*, 3 vols., vol. 1, p. 96.

7. "Disciple all nations" is a more literal translation of the Greek original *(mathēteusate panta ta ethnē)* than the more customary "make disciples of all nations." The more literal translation has the virtue of being more in keeping with the Old Testament's witness to Messiah's dominion over nations, rather than merely over scattered individuals within the nations.

the Spirit to empower that proclamation. Those nations that resist the authority of the resurrected and ascended Messiah are in danger of being broken in pieces with a rod of iron (2:9)—as was rebellious Israel in the destruction of Jerusalem (A.D. 70).

Psalm 22, another clearly messianic psalm, speaks of both the suffering and the subsequent exaltation of God's Anointed One. After giving a striking foreshadowing of the crucifixion of Christ in verses 16–18 (cf. Matt. 27:35), the psalmist then speaks of the redemptive impact of that suffering on the nations:

> All the ends of the earth shall remember
>   and turn to the LORD;
> and all the families of the nations
>   shall worship before him.
> For dominion belongs to the LORD,
>   and he rules over the nations. [vv. 27–28]

"The sufferer expects," note Keil and Delitzsch, as a result of the proclamation of what God has done for him, "the conversion of all peoples."[8] According to Henry the text indicates that the ultimate outcome of the sufferings of Christ here depicted will be that "the church of Christ, and with it the Kingdom of God among men, should extend itself to all corners of the earth."[9] It is the Father's will that, through the church's preaching of Christ crucified and risen, "all the families of the nations shall worship before him." Such references to "all the families of the nations" need to be understood not only in reference to the New Testament's Great Commission, but perhaps even more fundamentally against the background of the Abrahamic covenant and God's desire to bring spiritual bless-

---

8. Keil and Delitzsch, *The Psalms*, vol. 1, p. 324.
9. Matthew Henry, *Commentary on the Whole Bible*, ed. Leslie F. Church, 1-vol. ed. (Grand Rapids: Zondervan, 1961), pp. 599–600.

ings to "all the families of the earth" (Gen. 12:3). Reading
the texts in this light helps the New Testament believer to
avoid "minimalist" expectations concerning the ultimate
success of the Great Commission. God intends to bring not
merely scattered individuals, but multitudes, even nations, to worship at the throne of Jesus Christ.

The universal reign of God's Messiah is foretold in
Psalm 72, ascribed to Solomon:

> May he have dominion from sea to sea,
>   and from the River to the ends of the earth!
> May his foes bow down before him,
>   and his enemies lick the dust!
> May the kings of Tarshish and of the isles
>   render him tribute,
> may the kings of Sheba and Seba bring gifts!
> May all kings fall down before him,
>   all nations serve him! [vv. 8–11]

The Messiah's rule is clearly not restricted to Israel. God's
Anointed One is to have universal dominion; he is truly
"King of kings and Lord of lords" (Rev. 19:16). That universal dominion is already actual in a spiritual sense with
Christ now seated at the right hand of God, far above all
rule and authority and power and dominion, with all
things under his feet (Eph. 1:20–22), and is also in the
process of being actualized progressively in history as the
church preaches the gospel in the power of the Spirit—a
message with divine power to destroy strongholds (2 Cor.
10:4).

Perhaps the most important of the messianic psalms for
our purposes is Psalm 110, which speaks of the Messiah's
enthronement, and is frequently quoted by the New Testament writers:

> The LORD says to my lord:
> "Sit at my right hand,

> till I make your enemies
> your footstool."

> The LORD sends forth from Zion
> your mighty scepter.
> Rule in the midst of your foes! [vv. 1–2]

The Lord (God the Father) says to David's lord (God the Son, the Messiah, Jesus Christ), "Sit at my right hand, till I make your enemies your footstool." The apostle Peter declared on the day of Pentecost that Psalm 110:1 had been fulfilled in the resurrection and ascension of Jesus Christ. David, "knowing that God had sworn with an oath to him that he would set one of his descendants upon his throne, . . . foresaw and spoke of the resurrection of the Christ . . . . Being therefore exalted at the right hand of God, . . . he has poured out this [the Spirit] which you see and hear" (Acts 2:30, 31, 33). In verse 34 Peter specifically quotes Psalm 110:1 in relation to the resurrection and exaltation of Jesus as Lord and Messiah.

Thus the risen Christ is now at God's right hand, and is now in the process of subduing his foes. "Sitting at the right hand of God is a description taken from the judicial custom of the East and meant not only the highest honor thinkable but also unlimited participation in the world dominion of God. This heavenly act of solemn transfer introduces a new era in world history, the era of the kingdom of Christ over the whole world."[10]

The phrase *right hand of God* is a clear statement of the location from which Christ exercises his dominion. In the New Testament Christ's being at the right hand of God is uniformly understood in terms of his reign in heaven (Acts 2:33, 34; 5:31; 7:55–56; Rom. 8:34; Eph. 1:20; Col. 3:1; Heb.

---

10. *Herder's Commentary on the Psalms,* ed. Edmund Kalt, trans. Bernard Fritz (Westminster, Md.: Newman Press, 1961), p. 429.

1:3; 10:12; 1 Peter 3:22), and not in terms of a physical reign on earth.

Notice also the crucial adverbial particle *till* (*ad*, during, while, until) used here: "Sit at my right hand, *until* I make your enemies your footstool."[11] Christ remains in heaven while his foes are being subdued and until that process is complete.

This temporal reference has important implications for the believer's hopes for the success of Christ's cause in the present church age, prior to his physical return at the end of history. According to Psalm 110:1, Christ does not need to be physically present on earth to subdue his spiritual foes; this he does while still at the Father's right hand in heaven. Christ already has all power in heaven and on earth. As Keil and Delitzsch rightly note, "absolute omnipotence is effectual on behalf of and through the exalted Christ."[12] This invincible spiritual power is now available to the church in its mission to the world (Matt. 28:18–19; Eph. 1:19–20). The gates of hell itself cannot withstand the almighty spiritual power of the exalted Christ. It is this victorious and confident outlook that pervades Paul's understanding of Psalm 110:1 in 1 Corinthians 15:20–28, an important New Testament passage that will be examined in a subsequent chapter.

While Christ is still in heaven at the Father's right hand, God sends forth from Zion (the church, Heb. 12:22–23) his Son's mighty scepter (the gospel, the Word of God), that he might rule in the midst of his foes. Christ's heavenly reign is exercised and enlarged as the church on earth goes forth in the power of the Spirit to fulfill the Great Commission.

---

11. For further discussion of matters relating to the word *until* (*ad*), see J. J. Stewart Perowne, *The Book of Psalms*, 2 vols. (Andover: Warren F. Draper, 1894), vol. 2, p. 292.

12. Keil and Delitzsch, *The Psalms*, vol. 3, p. 190.

The Prophecies of Isaiah

The Book of Isaiah contains a number of prophecies that are of particular interest in relation to the postmillennial perspective. The first of these is found in 2:2–4, which speaks of the exaltation of Zion in the latter days:

> It shall come to pass in the latter days
>   that the mountain of the house of the LORD
> shall be established as the highest of the mountains,
>   and shall be raised above the hills;
> and all the nations shall flow to it,
>   and many peoples shall come, and say:
> "Come, let us go up to the mountain of the LORD,
>   to the house of the God of Jacob;
> that he may teach us his ways
>   and that we may walk in his paths."
> For out of Zion shall go forth the law,
>   and the word of the LORD from Jerusalem.
> He shall judge between the nations,
>   and shall decide for many peoples;
> and they shall beat their swords into plowshares,
>   and their spears into pruning hooks;
> nation shall not lift up sword against nation,
>   neither shall they learn war any more.

This famous passage is understood to refer to the latter-day spiritual exaltation of the Christian church, which is the true Zion and the heavenly Jerusalem (Heb. 12:22). A spiritually renewed church attracts the nations (v. 2) to the Christian faith by the vitality and depth of its worship, doctrine, and life. The noun *law* (v. 3), as Calvin points out, is a figure of speech which refers to the Word of God as a whole.[13] The pervasive impact of the gospel in the life of the nations produces a state of affairs where warfare and the production of its implements cease (v. 4).

---

13. John Calvin, *Commentary on the Book of the Prophet Isaiah*, trans. William Pringle, 4 vols. (Grand Rapids: Eerdmans, 1948), vol. 1, p. 96.

Isaiah states that such things are to take place in the "latter days." To what period of time is the prophet referring? As Edward J. Young has pointed out, the New Testament writers apply this phrase to the period of time which began with the first advent of Christ (Acts 2:17; Heb. 1:2; James 5:3; 1 Peter 1:5, 20; 2 Peter 3:3; 1 John 2:18).[14] In this sense the entire church age, the time between the first and second comings of Christ, constitutes the "last days." The events foretold in Isaiah 2:2–4 have already received limited, partial fulfillment through the church's missionary outreach and positive impact on civilization, and even more can be expected during a time of dramatic outpourings of the Holy Spirit in the life of the church.

It should be noted that Isaiah 2:2–4 makes no reference to a visible, physical presence of the Messiah, as though the second advent had already taken place. Neither is there a primary reference to the eternal, heavenly state since the reference to plowshares implies that the normal processes of agriculture will still be taking place. The "last days" are the period when Christ the Messiah is still at the right hand of the Father in heaven (Heb. 1:2–3), prior to the second advent and the final consummation.

Isaiah 9:6–7 is a famous prophecy of the birth of the messianic king:

> For to us a child is born,
>   to us a son is given;
> and the government will be upon his shoulder,
>   and his name will be called
> "Wonderful Counselor, Mighty God,
>   Everlasting Father, Prince of Peace."
> Of the increase of his government and of peace
>   there will be no end,
> upon the throne of David, and over his kingdom,
>   to establish it, and to uphold it

---

14. Edward J. Young, *The Book of Isaiah*, 3 vols. (Grand Rapids: Eerdmans, 1965), vol. 1, p. 98.

> with justice and with righteousness
>   from this time forth and for evermore.
> The zeal of the LORD of hosts will do this.

The prophet foresees the birth of no merely human messiah, but a truly divine deliverer, as the striking term *Mighty God* (v. 6) indicates. In Isaiah 10:21 this term clearly refers to Jehovah, the God of Israel. Isaiah 9:6–7 foretells the birth and subsequent rule of Jesus Christ, the divine Messiah and true heir of the throne of David.

Isaiah states that "of the increase of his government . . . there will be no end . . . from this time forth and for evermore." Calvin makes the comment that God not only protects and defends the kingdom of Christ, "but also extends its boundaries far and wide, and then preserves and carries it forward in uninterrupted progression to eternity."[15]

To what period of time does the phrase *from this time forth* (v. 7) refer? A natural way of understanding the phrase would be in relation to the time when the government is upon Messiah's shoulder (v. 6), and when he actually is reigning upon David's throne (v. 7). The New Testament shows that Jesus Christ, since the time of his resurrection and ascension to heaven at the right hand of the Father, has been reigning from the throne of David (Acts 2:30–31, 33–35). The increase of Christ's kingdom predicted by Isaiah has been in progress since his resurrection and will continue until the second advent and the consummation of all things (see 1 Cor. 15:23–24).

The eleventh chapter of Isaiah contains yet another well-known picture of the conditions of the messianic age:

> The wolf shall dwell with the lamb,
>   and the leopard shall lie down with the kid. . . .
> They shall not hurt or destroy
>   in all my holy mountain;

---

15. Calvin, *The Prophet Isaiah*, vol. 1, p. 313.

for the earth shall be full of the knowledge of the LORD
as the waters cover the sea.

In that day shall the root of Jesse stand as an ensign to
the peoples; him shall the nations seek, and his dwellings
shall be glorious. [vv. 6, 9–10]

In the postmillennial perspective the references to the
pacification of the animal kingdom are understood as figurative references to the dramatic changes in warring
human nature that can be produced by the gospel. Such
effects are to be more dramatically visible during the
latter-day glory of the church. Henry comments that a
"generation of vipers shall become a seed of saints."[16] Frequently in the Scriptures unruly and rebellious human
beings are referred to figuratively as animals: "You brood
of vipers" (Matt. 3:7, John the Baptist of the Pharisees and
Sadducees); "I fought with beasts at Ephesus" (1 Cor.
15:32, Paul of his opponents); see also Acts 20:29 and Matthew 7:15.

In that day, when the name of Christ is exalted in a
particularly powerful manner through the ministry of a
spiritually revitalized church, the nations will seek Christ
and his gospel, and the crucified One will draw all peoples
to himself (John 12:32) in a remarkable way.

The blessings of the church's latter-day glory spoken of
in Isaiah 11:6–9 are reiterated and expanded in Isaiah
65:17–25. The intensified period of spiritual blessing produces conditions in the world that are termed "new heavens and a new earth" (v. 17). This refers to the dramatic
moral renovation of society rather than to the eternal
state, since Isaiah speaks of a time when children are still
being born (v. 20), when people are still building houses
and planting vineyards (v. 21) and engaging in their

16. Henry, *Commentary on the Whole Bible*, p. 845.

earthly labors (v. 22). Paul uses similar language when he
says that salvation in Christ is like a "new creation"
(2 Cor. 5:17), or again in Galatians 6:15, "For neither cir-
cumcision counts for anything, nor uncircumcision, but a
new creation."

The conditions of health and temporal peace of which
Isaiah speaks in 65:17–25 are not the essence of the gospel, but they are properly the consequences of the gospel
when its impact is intensive and extensive in the world.
The message of reconciliation with God also produces as
its fruit reconciliation between man and man and even
with the natural order itself.

It should also be noted that 65:17–25 makes no reference to the Messiah's physical presence on earth. In the
latter days God desires to create in Jerusalem (the church)
a rejoicing (v. 18), but the realities of verses 18–25 refer
neither exclusively to the eternal state nor to the time
following the second advent, but rather to the messianic
age when Christ still rules at the right hand of the Father
in heaven.

Ezekiel's Vision: The River Flowing from the Temple

The forty-seventh chapter of the Book of Ezekiel contains a remarkable vision of a river flowing from the
threshold of the temple:

> Then he brought me back to the door of the temple; and
> behold, water was issuing from below the threshold of the
> temple toward the east. . . .
> Going on eastward with a line in his hand, the man
> measured a thousand cubits, and then led me through the
> water; and it was ankle-deep. . . . Again he measured a
> thousand, and it was a river that I could not pass through,
> for the water had risen. . . .

". . . and when it enters the stagnant waters of the sea, the water will become fresh. And wherever the river goes every living creature which swarms will live . . . ." [vv. 1, 3, 5, 8–9]

There are other references to "living waters" in the Old Testament (Joel 3:18; Zech. 14:8; cf. Ps. 46:4), but Ezekiel's description is by far the most extensive. What is the significance of this mysterious river which increases in such a miraculous way and brings life to all it touches?

The key to understanding Ezekiel's vision may be found in John 7:37–39, where Jesus, on the final day of the Feast of Tabernacles, stands up and proclaims:

"If any man thirst, let him come to me; and let him drink, who believes in me. As the scripture says, 'From his belly shall flow rivers of living water.'"[17] Now this he said about *the Spirit,* which those who believed in him were to receive . . . [italics added].

On each day of the Feast of Tabernacles, a priest took a golden flask holding about four-and-a-half pints of water from the pool of Siloam near Jerusalem, carried it through the Water Gate, went up the ramp to the altar, and poured it out.[18] The pilgrims who observed this ritual would likely have associated this water ceremony with the eschatological outpouring of water in Ezekiel's vision.[19] On

17. This translation of the quotation is based on the punctuation found in Western manuscripts. See Bruce Grigsby, "Gematria and John 21:11: Another Look at Ezekiel 47:10," *Expository Times* 95:6 (1984):177–78, and Raymond E. Brown, *The Gospel According to John* (i–xii) (Garden City, N.Y.: Doubleday, 1966), pp. 320–31, who also supports this translation.

18. See Mishnah *Succah* 4:9, 10 in *Mishnayoth*, trans. Philip Blackman, 7 vols. (New York: Judaica Press, 1963), vol. 2, pp. 339–40. For further background on the Feast of Tabernacles, see George W. MacRae, "The Meaning and Evolution of the Feast of Tabernacles," *Catholic Biblical Quarterly* 22 (1960): 251–76.

19. Grigsby, "Gematria and John 21:11," p. 177; Brown also points to Exod. 17, the incident of the water from the rock in the wilderness, as another likely Old Testament background for John 7:37–39.

this understanding, Jesus is here deliberately presenting himself as the fulfillment of Ezekiel's prophecy. In John's Gospel Jesus presents himself as the true temple of God (2:19–21), water is associated with the Spirit (3:5; 4:13–14, 23–24), and Jesus sends the Spirit to his disciples (7:39; 16:7).

Ezekiel's vision, then, finds its fulfillment in Jesus Christ, the true temple of God, who, after his death, resurrection, and ascension to the right hand of God, sends forth rivers of life-giving water—the Holy Spirit—upon his people (Acts 2:33, "Being therefore exalted at the right hand of God, . . . he has poured out this which you see and hear"). Ezekiel's prophecy looks forward to Pentecost and the subsequent outpourings of the Spirit during the church age. The imagery of the ever-deepening river implies that Pentecost was only the beginning: God has yet greater effusions of the Spirit in store for mankind. The Spirit of God, poured out in great abundance upon the church and through the church into the world, is destined to bring as yet unimagined blessings to the human race.[20]

Daniel's Visions

The second and seventh chapters of the Book of Daniel contain visions which are directly relevant to a discussion of postmillennialism. In Daniel 2:31–35 Daniel relates the contents of King Nebuchadnezzar's dream, in which he saw a great image destroyed by a mysterious stone of supernatural origin:

"You saw, O king, and behold, a great image. . . . The head of this image was of fine gold, its breast and arms of silver,

---

20. Walther Zimmerli, *Ezekiel 2* (Philadelphia: Fortress, 1983), p. 513, points to a similarity between Ezekiel's vision of the river and Jesus' parables of growth in the New Testament: small beginnings end with remarkably great results.

its belly and thighs of bronze, its legs of iron, its feet partly
of iron and partly of clay. As you looked, a stone was cut out
by no human hand, and it smote the image on its feet of
iron and clay, and broke them in pieces; then the iron, the
clay, the bronze, the silver, and the gold, all together were
broken in pieces, and became like the chaff of the summer
threshing floors; and the wind carried them away, so that
not a trace of them could be found. But the stone that
struck the image became a great mountain and filled the
whole earth."

In Daniel's interpretation of the dream the image is understood in terms of the succession of earthly kingdoms, and
the mysterious stone which destroys them is identified
with the kingdom of God (v. 44). Elsewhere in Scripture a
stone is associated with the divine presence (Num. 20:8;
Deut. 32:4; Isa. 8:14; 17:10; 44:8; 51:1).[21]

The Aramaic term used only here in verses 34 and 35
and rendered "strike" or "smite" has a Hebrew equivalent
which can mean "clapping the hands" (Ps. 98:8; Isa. 55:12;
Ezek. 25:6). The context of the passage seems to imply a
process of repeated blows,[22] and the vision emphasizes the
completeness of the demolition of the image ("like chaff
. . . and the wind carried them away," v. 35).

As early as Jerome, Christian interpreters have understood the four kingdoms symbolized by the image as the
Babylonian, Medeo-Persian, Greek, and Roman em-

---

21. Andre Lacocque, *The Book of Daniel,* trans. David Pellauer (Atlanta:
John Knox, 1978), p. 49.

22. Albert Barnes, *Notes . . . on Daniel* (New York: Leavitt and Allen, 1853),
p. 135. Boutflower points out that Daniel's Babylonian audience would have
been especially impressed by the dream and Daniel's interpretation, since in
Babylonian mythology Enlil, the Most High God, was associated with a great
mountain. The implication of the dream was that the dominion attributed to
Enlil was in fact fulfilled in Daniel's God, the true God of heaven. Charles
Boutflower, *In and Around the Book of of Daniel* (Grand Rapids: Zondervan,
1963), pp. 45–54.

pires.[23] Jesus Christ is the living stone, rejected by men but chosen by God (1 Peter 2:4) and now the head of the corner (Acts 4:11), who comes from heaven to defeat all earthly opposition. The kingdom of Jesus Christ, inaugurated during the Roman Empire, overcame it against all human odds, and is destined to expand until it fills the entire earth (Dan. 2:35). The picture of the victorious expansion of the kingdom of Christ is consistent with Christ's own parables of the growth of the kingdom (Matt. 13:31–33, the mustard seed and the leaven). Small and unlikely beginnings eventuate in the universal victory of the kingdom of Christ.

In the seventh chapter Daniel recounts a vision of a heavenly "son of man":

> I saw in the night visions,
>> and behold, with the clouds of heaven
>>> there came one like a son of man,
>> and he came to the Ancient of Days
>>> and was presented before him.
> And to him was given dominion
>> and glory and kingdom,
> that all peoples, nations, and languages
>> should serve him;
> his dominion is an everlasting dominion,
>> which shall not pass away,
> and his kingdom one
>> that shall not be destroyed. [vv. 13–14]

In Matthew 26:64 Jesus clearly identifies himself with this mysterious figure in Daniel 7. After his betrayal and arrest, Jesus says to Caiaphas, the high priest, "Hereafter

---

23. *Jerome's Commentary on Daniel,* trans. Gleason L. Archer, Jr. (Grand Rapids: Baker, 1958), pp. 31–32. Modern critical commentators, who tend to assume a second-century, Maccabean date for Daniel, frequently identify the four kingdoms with the Babylonian, Median, Persian, and Greek empires. See, for example, Raymond Hammer, *The Book of Daniel* (Cambridge: Cambridge University Press, 1976), p. 32.

you will see the Son of man seated at the right hand of Power, and coming on the clouds of heaven." Caiaphas understood this statement as a claim to be a divine Messiah and responded, "He has uttered *blasphemy*" (Matt. 26:65, italics added).

Stephen, the first Christian martyr, also understood Jesus to be the Son of man of Daniel 7. At the conclusion of his discourse before the Jewish leaders, and immediately prior to his death, Stephen gazed into heaven, saw Jesus standing at the right hand of God, and said, "Behold, I see the heavens opened, and the Son of man standing at the right hand of God" (Acts 7:56). In the Book of Revelation Christ is described as one "coming with the clouds" (Rev. 1:7; cf. 14:14), as is the Son of man in Daniel. From the perspective of the New Testament it is clear that the heavenly Son of man in Daniel 7 is none other than Jesus Christ himself.[24]

Where is the scene in Daniel's vision taking place—in heaven or on earth? Alexander A. Di Lella points out that the Aramaic words in verse 13, "and was presented before him," are the same ones used in the fifth-century B.C. Aramaic story of Ahiqar: "I brought you into the presence of King Sennacherib." The idea involved is that of a royal audience.[25] The Son of man in the vision did not descend from God as if he had been an angel in the divine presence, "but rather he ascended or came to God and was brought into his presence."[26] Daniel 7:13 is thus a vision of the

---

24. Critical scholars generally deny that the "Son of man" in Daniel 7 is a personal messiah and argue that the figure is a symbol of Israel or the righteous remnant of Israel. See, for example, Sigmund Mowinckel, *He That Cometh: The Messiah Concept in the Old Testament and Later Judaism*, trans. G. W. Anderson (New York: Abingdon, 1956), p. 350. For analysis and criticism of this nonmessianic view of Dan. 7:13, see Boutflower, *In and Around the Book of Daniel*, pp. 55–65.

25. Alexander A. Di Lella, "The One in Human Likeness and the Holy Ones of the Most High in Daniel 7," *Catholic Biblical Quarterly* 39:1 (1977): 19.

26. Ibid. G. R. Beasley-Murray, "The Interpretation of Daniel 7," *Catholic Biblical Quarterly* 45:1 (1983): 49, thinks that the scene takes place on earth, but admits that most exegetes favor the heavenly location.

ascension of Christ. This understanding is consistent with Jesus' reference in Matthew 26:64 to being at the "right hand of Power" and Stephen's vision of the resurrected Christ now at the "right hand of God" (Acts 7:56; cf. Acts 2:33, "exalted at the right hand of God").

The heavenly Son of man—the ascended Christ—is given dominion that "all peoples, nations, and languages should serve him" (7:14). This dominion is now being realized in the church age as the church obeys the Great Commission mandate to preach the gospel and to disciple all nations.

The visions in Daniel 2 and Daniel 7 can thus be seen as different aspects of the same marvelous reality: the expanding, victorious kingdom of the risen Christ. Daniel 2 describes this expansion from the viewpoint of earthly history, while Daniel 7:13–14 points to the heavenly, exalted Christ who is directing and empowering the expansion of his kingdom from the throne room of God.

3

The Witness
of the New Testament

C hrist's monarchic rule 'over all' makes not
only all angelic and demonic powers (1:21f.), but also all
men—whether they know it and like it—subject to the
terms of his dominion," comments Markus Barth on Ephesians 1:19–22.[1] This recognition of the universal dominion
of the risen and ascended Christ is a fitting introduction to
a consideration of the New Testament witness in relation
to the postmillennial perspective. As noted earlier, the
postmillennial outlook is not so much a matter of chro-
nology as it is of Christology—a focus on the grandeur and
the power of the ascended Lord and the greatness of his
power that is available to the church in its mission. Our
discussion in this chapter will be organized along the following lines: first, texts pointing to the greatness of Christ
the King; second, texts describing the growth of Christ's

---

1. Markus Barth, *The Broken Wall: A Study of the Epistle to the Ephesians*
(Chicago: Judson, 1959), pp. 55–56.

kingdom; and third, texts highlighting the final greatness
of Christ's kingdom.

The Greatness of Christ the King

"All authority in heaven and on earth has been given to
me" (Matt. 28:18). This astonishing declaration by Christ
to his disciples is made after the resurrection and prior to
the ascension. Prior to the cross Jesus came in the form of
a servant (Phil. 2:7), but now he manifests himself as
the almighty Lord from heaven. *Exousia* denotes active
power, the full ability to do as one wills.[2] The expression *in
heaven and on earth* indicates totality and comprehensiveness. Christ here asserts a universal and plenipotenti-
ary authority; nothing could be more comprehensive.
"Never did a human army have such resources behind it,"
writes R. C. H. Lenski. "All the earth is also subject to
him, its inhabitants, both friend and foe, and all the
powers that are in the earth."[3] It is precisely in the light of
this unlimited authority that Christ sends his disciples
into the world as the agents of his kingdom, not in the
strength of their own human resources, but energized
with a divine authority that is his alone.

The gift of the Holy Spirit on the day of Pentecost was a
powerful reminder and attestation to the disciples of the
Lord's exaltation and power. "Being therefore *exalted* at
the right hand of God, . . . he has poured out this which
you see and hear," Peter declared (Acts 2:33, italics added).
The apostle then cited Psalm 110:1, "The Lord said to my
Lord, Sit at my right hand, till I make thy enemies a stool
for thy feet" (vv. 34–35).[4] "Let all the house of Israel therefore know assuredly," said Peter, "that God has made him

---

2. R. C. H. Lenski, *The Interpretation of St. Matthew's Gospel* (Columbus,
Ohio: Wartburg, 1943), p. 1171.

3. Ibid.

4. On the use of Ps. 110 in the early church, see David M. Hay, *Glory at the
Right Hand: Psalm 110 in Early Christianity* (Nashville: Abingdon, 1973).

both Lord and Christ, this Jesus whom you crucified" (v. 36). The crucified one now reigns from heaven, sending forth the Spirit for the growth and empowerment of the church.

Perhaps the most sublime description of the risen Christ's exalted authority is found in Ephesians 1:19–23, where the apostle prays that the Ephesian believers might experience a deeper grasp of the

> immeasurable greatness of his power in us who believe, according to the working of his great might which he accomplished in Christ when he raised him from the dead and made him sit at his right hand in the heavenly places, far above all rule and authority and power and dominion, and above every name that is named, not only in this age but also in that which is to come; and he has put all things under his feet and has made him the head over all things for the church, which is his body, the fulness of him who fills all in all.

This magnificent description of the present reign of Christ can be seen as the "heavenly" counterpart to the words of Jesus in Matthew 28:18, "all authority in heaven and on earth has been given to me." A more comprehensive claim for the authority and power of Christ could hardly be imagined.

In verse 19 Paul ransacks the Greek language to stress the mighty power of Christ, piling synonym upon synonym. "He calls it not only great power," notes Thomas Goodwin, "but 'greatness of power,' and not content with that, it is *to huperballon megethos,* the exceeding, super-excelling, sublime, overcoming, triumphing greatness of his power."[5] The power *(dunamis)* of God which Paul stresses is not just an abstract quality, but a reality which

---

5. Thomas Goodwin, *An Exposition of Ephesians* (reprint ed.; Evansville, Ind.: Sovereign Grace Book Club, 1958), p. 332.

is known according to its working and can be seen and realized.[6] The great might *(kratos)* referred to is something overcoming and prevailing; "it is a conquering, prevailing greatness of his power that is able to subdue all things," writes Goodwin.[7]

Paul discloses this astonishing vision of the ascended Christ not as a theoretical theological exercise, but in order to challenge the believing church to appropriate this mighty spiritual power in its inner life and mission to the world. "The Church has authority and power to overcome all opposition," as Francis Foulkes rightly observes, "because her Leader and Head is Lord of all."[8]

The same power that raised Christ from the dead (v. 20) is available, through faith, to believers as they obey the Great Commission. Like other New Testament writers, Paul sees Jesus exalted at the right hand of God (v. 20b; Ps. 110:1), with all things under his feet (v. 22; Ps. 8:6), reigning supreme over all the spiritual beings that would oppose the victorious kingdom of God. God has made him head over all things for the church (v. 22). This is the Christ who has "disarmed" the principalities and powers, publicly leading them chained in his triumphant victory parade (Col. 2:15),[9] and who has gone into heaven, with angels, authorities, and powers subject to him (1 Peter 3:22; Heb. 2:5–9).

There is the greatest possible encouragement here for those who go forth in the name of Christ to evangelize the world. The authority and power of Christ are far above every name that can be named (v. 21)—far above that of

---

6. Francis Foulkes, *The Epistle of Paul to the Ephesians: An Introduction and Commentary* (Grand Rapids: Eerdmans, 1963), p. 62.

7. Goodwin, *An Exposition of Ephesians*, p. 333.

8. Foulkes, *The Epistle of Paul to the Ephesians*, p. 65.

9. On Col. 2:15, see J. B. Lightfoot, *Saint Paul's Epistles to the Colossians and to Philemon* (London: Macmillan, 1882), p. 192. The allusion here is most likely to the common practice of Roman generals returning in triumph, parading the conquered enemy soldiers in chains through the streets of Rome.

Muhammad, Buddha, Krishna, Marx, or any others that might oppose the Christian faith. The most serious obstacle to the success of the church's mission is not the power of its spiritual opponents, but the church's own weakness of faith and partial grasp of the invincible resources which are hers in Christ Jesus.

The Growth of the Kingdom

The parables of growth in Matthew 13:31–33 are Christ's own description and prophecy of the amazing growth and vitality of the kingdom he came to establish:

> "The kingdom of heaven is like a grain of mustard seed which a man took and sowed in his field; it is the smallest of all seeds, but when it has grown it is the greatest of shrubs and becomes a tree, so that the birds of the air come and make nests in its branches. . . . The kingdom of heaven is like leaven which a woman took and hid in three measures of flour, till it all was leavened."[10]

These images of dramatic growth recall the mysterious stone from heaven that grew into a great mountain (Dan. 2:35) and the miraculous river of water from the temple that increased in depth and width apart from all human agency (Ezek. 47:1–12).

The mustard seed was the smallest garden-variety seed known to people in biblical times. "Small as a grain of mustard seed" was a proverbial expression among the Jews for something minute (cf. Luke 17:6, "If you had faith as a grain of mustard seed").[11] The plant referred to may have been the *Sinapis nigra* or "black mustard," which

---

10. These parables of the kingdom are also found in Mark 4:30–32 and Luke 13:18–19.

11. Richard C. Trench, *Notes on the Parables of Our Lord* (New York: N. Tibbals and Sons, 1879), p. 91.

was cultivated to produce mustard and oil.[12] The seed of
one variety of the mustard plant is only one millimeter
(.039 inch) across.[13]

The varieties of the mustard plant found in Palestine
are annuals and shoot up in a relatively short time, high
above the other vegetables. In warmer regions and in rich
soil they grow to a great size and the lower part of the stalk
becomes quite woody.[14] In Palestine the mustard plant
can grow to a height of eight to twelve feet.[15]

This parable focuses on the kingdom in its visible
growth. "The kingdom," writes Lenski, "is like a mustard
kernel because, like it, the rule of Christ's grace among
men has a phenomenal growth from the tiniest beginning." This is a growth which continues throughout
time.[16] As such, the parable is a great source of encouragement to the disciples' faith. From small and insignificant
beginnings truly remarkable growth will surely come.

The parable of the leaven is also an illustration of the
growth of the kingdom, but from a different aspect. Here
the inward, secret working of the kingdom and its pervasive influence are in view. Leaven is an illustration of
the "mighty, all-penetrating force of the kingdom of
God."[17]

"Three measures" were evidently a customary quantity
for a substantial meal (see Gen. 18:6). Some interpreters

---

12. J. A. Sproule, "The Problem of the Mustard Seed," *Grace Theological Journal* 1 (1980): 37–42. On the botanical identification of the plant referred to in the parable, see also G. Granata, "La 'sinapis' del Vangelo," *Bibliotheca Orientalis* 24 (1982): 175–77, and G. Pace, "La senepa del Vangelo," *Bibliotheca Orientalis* 22 (1980): 119–23.

13. Robert G. Bratcher, *A Translator's Guide to the Gospel of Mark* (London: United Bible Societies, 1981), p. 51, on Mark 4:31.

14. Leopold Fonck, *The Parables of the Gospel: An Exegetical and Practical Explanation* (New York: Frederick Pustet Co., 1914), p. 161.

15. Harvey K. McArthur, "The Parable of the Mustard Seed," *Catholic Biblical Quarterly* 33 (1971): 201.

16. Lenski, *The Interpretation of St. Matthew's Gospel*, pp. 527, 529, 530.

17. Fonck, *The Parables of the Gospel*, p. 177. "Three measures" involved more than a bushel of flour—a substantial amount.

have seen the leaven as a symbol of evil (see 1 Cor. 5:7; Luke 12:1; Gal. 5:9). In this view the parable would be an illustration of the "leavening" of the church with false teaching. But this construction is contrary to the explicit words of Jesus: "The kingdom of heaven is like leaven" (v. 33). Christ and the power of his life, death, resurrection, and teaching—not false doctrine—are clearly the point of the saying. Elsewhere in the New Testament the same figure can be used in diverse senses, for example, a lion as symbolic of the devil in one text (1 Peter 5:8) and of Christ in another (Rev. 5:5). The context must be decisive for the proper interpretation in any given instance.

The parable of the leaven, like that of the mustard seed, teaches an optimistic and hopeful message that is an encouragement to faith. It shows, notes Lenski, that "the gospel cannot but *succeed,* and the one work of the church is to preach, teach, and spread it in the world. The parable teaches faith, patience, hope, and joy."[18]

Both parables describe the small and insignificant beginnings, the gradual progress, and the final marvelous increase of the church.[19] "Nor can we consider these words, *'till the whole is leavened,'*" writes Richard C. Trench, "as less than a prophecy of a final complete triumph of the Gospel—that it will diffuse itself through all nations, and purify and ennoble all life."[20] This hopeful vision of the ultimate outcome of Christian mission is consistent with the immutable redemptive intention of God to bring spiritual blessings to "all the families of the earth" (Gen. 12:3).

These two pictures of the growth of the kingdom formed a striking contrast with the messianic expectations which were common in Judaism during the first century. "One wave of the magic wand was to accomplish everything in

---

18. R. C. H. Lenski, *The Interpretation of St. Luke's Gospel* (Columbus, Ohio: Wartburg, 1946), p. 745.
19. Trench, *Notes on the Parables of Our Lord,* p. 88.
20. Ibid., p. 90.

the twinkling of an eye," observes Frederic Godet. "In opposition to this superficial notion, Jesus sets the idea of a moral development which works by spiritual means and takes account of human freedom, consequently slow and progressive."[21]

Much twentieth-century biblical scholarship has stressed the apocalyptic features of the New Testament. This point of view would focus on the dramatic and cataclysmic nature of the kingdom, and stress discontinuity rather than continuity and gradual progress. The parables of the mustard seed and the leaven are good reminders of the fact that in our Lord's own mind, the kingdom of God is not to grow and triumph dramatically just at the end of history, but is to exhibit an amazing visible growth throughout history as well. The growth of the universal church may not be even in all ages and locations, but nevertheless, growth remains a basic characteristic of the kingdom of Christ—and this is a great source of encouragement and hope of those directly involved in missionary outreach.

The parables of the leaven and the mustard seed describe the nature and the remarkable extent of the growth of the kingdom; the Great Commission points to the means by which that growth is to be realized in history.

"*All authority* in heaven and on earth has been given to me," said Jesus to his disciples after the resurrection (Matt. 28:18, italics added). "Go therefore and make disciples of all nations" (Matt. 28:19).

Lenski points out that here the word *therefore (oun)* has particular force. "It puts all [Christ's] power and authority behind the commission to evangelize the world. The *oun* shows that what would be otherwise absolutely impossible now becomes gloriously possible, yea, an assured real-

---

21. Frederic Godet, *A Commentary on the Gospel of St. Luke,* trans. M. D. Cusin, 5th ed., 2 vols. (reprint ed.; Edinburgh: T. and T. Clark, 1976), vol. 2, p. 122.

ity."[22] And John Calvin observes, "The apostles would
never have been persuaded to attempt so arduous a task,
had they not known that their Protector and Avenger was
sitting in the heavens, to whom supreme dominion had
been given."[23]

To "make a disciple" is to bring a person into the relation of pupil to teacher, "tak[ing] the yoke" of authoritative
teaching (Matt. 11:29), accepting what the master says as
true out of personal trust for the teacher, and submitting
to the master's requirements as right because he makes
them.[24] *Mathēteusate* is an aorist imperative. The aorist
form conveys the thought that the command in question is
actually to be accomplished; it designates an activity that
will result in disciples.[25]

The universality of the commission is made clear by the
reference to *ta ethnē* (v. 19), "all nations" of the earth. Here
"all people groups" or "all ethnic groups" would be a better
translation, since for the modern reader "nation" denotes
a nation-state, a politically defined entity, rather than a
linguistically defined ethnic grouping.[26] Thus the one
nation-state of India is composed of a multitude of people
groups, which may be culturally isolated from one another. The presence of a Christian church within a nation-
state does not mean that all peoples within that political
unit are being evangelized. Christ's command to the
church is not merely that the gospel be preached within all
nation-states, but that all the people groups of the earth be
discipled through his teachings and divine authority.

22. Lenski, *The Interpretation of St. Matthew's Gospel*, p. 1172.
23. Cited in John A. Broadus, *Commentary on the Gospel of Matthew*
(Philadelphia: American Baptist Publication Society, 1886), p. 593.
24. Ibid.
25. Lenski, *The Interpretation of St. Matthew's Gospel*, p. 1172.
26. For a biblical example of this important distinction see, for example,
Esther 3:8: "Then Haman said to King Ahasuerus, 'There is a certain *people*
[people group; LXX, *ethnos*] scattered abroad and dispersed among the peoples
in all the provinces of your *kingdom* [political entity; LXX, *basileia*]; their laws
are different from those of every other people."

In the Great Commission, notes Lenski, "we have the fulfillment of all the Messianic promises concerning the coming kingdom."[27] The Great Commission is the New Testament form of the Abrahamic covenant, intended to bring blessing to all nations, and is the means by which that covenant is to be realized in history. The church can go forth joyously into the world with the conviction that its missionary activity fulfills the eternal redemptive purposes of God and will be blessed with the supernatural power and invincible authority of the risen Christ himself, who is with his people even to the end of the age (Matt. 28:20).

The hope of the church's ultimate victory over all the enemies of the gospel does not obscure the fact that in history the representatives of Christ encounter fierce conflict and opposition to their missionary endeavors. But Christ assures his people that even the "gates of Hades" *(pulai haidou)* can not prevail against the church (Matt. 16:18). "Hades," the unseen world, is here viewed as a mighty fortress, the opposite of the sacred temple of Christ. The expression *gates* (or, portals; *pulai*) *of Hades* is a figure for the warring demonic hosts that issue from below in order to assault the church.[28] The implication of the text, according to Lenski, is that "hell's gates shall pour out her hosts to assault the church of Christ, but the church shall not be overthrown . . . What makes her impregnable is her mighty foundation, Christ, the Son of the living God."[29]

The apostle Paul certainly experienced opposition of all sorts during his missionary labors, and yet he was confident of victory because of the spiritual power of Christ that was his. In the context of opposition from false apostles (2 Cor. 11:12–15), Paul in 2 Corinthians 10:3–5 re-

---

27. Lenski, *The Interpretation of St. Matthew's Gospel*, p. 1173.
28. Ibid., p. 628.
29. Ibid.

minds the Corinthian believers that his ministry is not dependent on merely human power:

> For though we live in the world we are not carrying on a worldly war, for the weapons of our warfare are not worldly but have divine power to destroy strongholds. We destroy arguments and every proud obstacle to the knowledge of God, and take every thought captive to obey Christ. . . .

Paul was convinced that the spiritual weapon of his own ministry—truth, righteousness, evangelism, faith, salvation, the Word of God, prayer (Eph. 6:14–17)—had "divine power to destroy strongholds" (v. 4). Today's missionary facing the "strongholds" of Islam, Hinduism, Buddhism, Marxism, secularism, and so forth can have the same confidence.

The apostle Paul was not intimidated "by the number, the authority, the ability, or the learning of his opponents," commented Charles Hodge. "He was confident that he could cast down all their proud imaginations because he relied not on himself but on God whose messenger he was."[30]

"There is no reason . . . for Christ's servant to tremble before any opposition to his teaching, however formidable," wrote Calvin. "Let him persevere in spite of it and he will put all sorts of machinations to flight."[31]

The apostle knew, like the apostle John, that "he who is in you is greater than he who is in the world" (1 John 4:4). Paul's confidence in the spiritual power of the gospel was no idle dream, for in less than three centuries the Roman Empire was conquered by these spiritual weapons, and the

---

30. Charles Hodge, *An Exposition of the Second Epistle to the Corinthians* (1859; Grand Rapids: Baker, 1980), p. 236.

31. John Calvin, *The Second Epistle of Paul the Apostle to the Corinthians and the Epistles to Timothy, Titus, and Philemon,* ed. David W. Torrance and Thomas F. Torrance, trans. T. A. Smail (Grand Rapids: Eerdmans, 1964), p. 130, on 2 Cor. 10:4.

emperor himself had become a Christian. "This war," noted Lenski, "could not lead to anything but victory."[32]

The ultimate source of the church's growth and missionary expansion is the ascended Christ, who *now* reigns over the church and the world from the Father's right hand, and even now is in the process of subduing his foes. This crucial witness to the present, active kingship of Christ is found, for example, in 1 Corinthians 15:22–26, an important passage for the postmillennial outlook. Paul speaks of Christ's active reign in the context of a discussion about the final resurrection of believers:

> For as in Adam all die, so also in Christ shall all be made alive. But each in his own order: Christ the first fruits, then at his coming *(parousia)* those who belong to Christ. Then comes the end *(eita to telos),* when he delivers the kingdom to God the Father after destroying every rule and every authority and power. For he must reign until he has put all his enemies under his feet. The last enemy *(eschatos echthros)* to be destroyed is death.

Several important questions of interpretation arise here in relation to the sequence of events that Paul describes. When Christ returns at the second advent to raise the dead (v. 23), Paul says that "then comes the end" *(eita to telos,* v. 24), when the Son then hands the kingdom over to the Father. Does the phrase *then comes the end* imply an interval of indefinite duration (a thousand years? [Rev. 20:4–6]) between the second coming and the "end," after all spiritual opposition has been subdued? Or is the *parousia* coterminous with the "end"?

In verse 25 Paul states that Christ must reign *until* all his foes have been subdued—a clear allusion to Psalm 110:1, so frequently quoted elsewhere in the New Testament. Where does this reigning and subduing take

---

32. R. C. H. Lenski, *The Interpretation of St. Paul's First and Second Epistles to the Corinthians* (Minneapolis: Augsburg, 1961), p. 1206.

place—in heaven, at the right hand of God, or on earth, after the second advent, during a millennial reign? Postmillennial and premillennial interpreters answer these questions in different ways.

In the first place it should be noted that in the New Testament "then" *(eita)* does not necessarily imply a long interval of time between the preceeding clause and that which it introduces (John 13:4–5; 19:26–27; 1 Cor. 15:5–7).[33] More specifically, in this very epistle Paul clearly understands the "end" to be coterminous with the second coming: "as you wait for the *revealing* of our Lord Jesus Christ; who will sustain you to the *end (telos)*, guiltless in the *day of our Lord Jesus Christ*" (1 Cor. 1:7–8, italics added). The "day of the Lord" is clearly the day of the second coming, as may be seen from 1 Thessalonians 5:2, "the day of the Lord will come like a thief in the night." The point is that the "end" does not come, say, a thousand years after the second coming; for Paul, the second coming *is* the end.

According to verse 24, then, we are to understand that the second coming occurs after Christ has destroyed "every rule and authority and power." Christ is now reigning in heaven at the Father's right hand and now is in the process of subduing his foes. This is the point of Paul's quotation of Psalm 110:1 in verse 25: Christ rules from heaven *until* all foes but death itself are subdued; then at the second coming, the *resurrection* shows that even death itself is overthrown (v. 26, "the last enemy"). Only then does Christ hand over the kingdom to the Father.

God delegates his kingship to Christ for a definite period, "from the raising of Christ . . . to his parousia, and for a definite end, the annihilation of the hostile powers," as Hans Conzelmann has correctly noted. "Now is already

---

33. W. D. Davies, *Paul and Rabbinic Judaism* (London: S.P.C.K., 1955), p. 293.

the time of the sovereignty of Christ, and therewith also of the subjecting of the powers."[34]

Similarly, C. K. Barrett states that there is "nothing to suggest that this developing reign of Christ falls between the *parousia* and the End; it culminates in the *parousia*."[35] As J. Lambrecht points out, the "sitting at the right hand of God" in heaven (v. 25; Ps. 110:1) is interpreted by Paul as Christ's active reigning on earth.[36] The only other Pauline text which speaks of the kingdom of the Son *(basileia tou huiou)* regards this kingdom as a present fact (Col. 1:12–13), not a kingdom to be established after the parousia.[37]

The apostle Paul, then, in this crucial passage opens up a vision for the church of Christ's ongoing spiritual triumphs in the present age. As Benjamin B. Warfield correctly noted, in a passage previously cited, this text describes

> the nature of the whole dispensation in which we are living, and which stretches from the First to the Second Advent, as a period of advancing conquest on the part of Christ. During its course He is to conquer "every rulership and every authority and power" (verse 24), and "to place all

---

34. Hans Conzelmann, *1 Corinthians: A Commentary on the First Epistle to the Corinthians,* ed. George W. MacRae, trans. James W. Leitch (Philadelphia: Fortress, 1975), p. 271.

35. C. K. Barrett, *A Commentary on the First Epistle to the Corinthians* (New York: Harper and Row, 1968), p. 357.

36. J. Lambrecht, "Paul's Christological Use of Scripture in 1 Cor. 15:20–28," *New Testament Studies* 28 (1982): 506; see also W. R. G. Loader, "Christ at the Right Hand—Ps. 110:1 in the New Testament," *New Testament Studies* 24 (1978): 208; Jean Hering, *The First Epistle of Saint Paul to the Corinthians* (London: Epworth, 1962), pp. 167–68, and Lenski, *First and Second Epistles to the Corinthians,* p. 672, for similar understandings of the present, heavenly reign of Christ, and the absence of any "millennial insert" between 1 Cor. 15:23b and 24. W. B. Wallis, "The Problem of an Intermediate Kingdom in 1 Corinthians 15:20–28," *Evangelical Theological Society Journal* 18 (1975): 229–42, argues for such a premillennial understanding, but overlooks the force of 1 Cor. 1:8 ("end" = second coming) in this connection.

37. Davies, *Paul and Rabbinic Judaism,* p. 296.

his enemies under His feet" (verse 25), and it ends when His conquests complete themselves by the subjugation of the "last enemy," death . . . the essence of Paul's representation is not that Christ is striving against evil, but progressively . . . overcoming evil, throughout this period.[38]

The period between the two advents is the period of Christ's victorious kingship, and when he comes again it is not to institute his kingdom, but to lay it down at the Father's feet.[39]

If Matthew 28:19–20 is the missionary mandate, 1 Corinthians 15:22–26 is a "golden text" of encouragement and hope for evangelical missions. The church does not have to wait until Christ is physically present on earth to expect substantial victory in the face of its spiritual foes. Christ, the almighty King, reigns in heaven now, and his invincible power is available to the church in its mission— if only believers will by faith lay hold of the exceedingly great spiritual resources which are theirs (Eph. 1:19–23). Paul's Christology is the key to his vision of Christian history, and sharing that vision can energize Christian missions in as yet unimagined ways.

The Final Greatness of the Kingdom

We have seen, then, the New Testament's witness to the greatness of the King, the resurrected and ascended Christ, and to the dramatic, supernatural growth of the kingdom—both foreshadowed in the messianic texts of the Old Testament. It now remains to note the New Testament's witness to the final greatness of the kingdom—the astounding spiritual harvest that is to fulfill God's global redemptive intent announced in the Abrahamic covenant and the Great Commission.

---

38. Benjamin B. Warfield, "The Prophecies of St. Paul," in *Biblical and Theological Studies*, ed. Samuel G. Craig (Philadelphia: Presbyterian and Reformed, 1952), p. 485.

39. Ibid., p. 487.

In John's Gospel Jesus, looking ahead to the crucifixion, declares, "I, when I am lifted up from the earth, will draw all men to myself" (12:32). This is not a statement of universal salvation (universalism), but it does announce the global scope and comprehensiveness of God's redemptive plan. This language is consistent with the promise of blessings for "all the families of the earth" (Gen. 12:3) and a spiritual progeny for Abraham as countless as the stars of heaven and the sand of the seashore (Gen. 22:17).

The author of the Book of Revelation is given a magnificent vision of the final harvest of God's redemptive work. The results are vast indeed (Rev. 7:9–10):

> After this I looked, and behold, a great multitude which no man could number, from every nation, from all tribes and peoples and tongues, standing before the throne and before the Lamb, clothed in white robes, with palm branches in their hands, and crying out with a loud voice, "Salvation belongs to our God who sits upon the throne, and to the Lamb!"

This is clearly a picture of those who have been truly saved, as the language of "salvation" in verse 10 indicates, and the number passes comprehension. "In every direction they stretch out as far as the eye can see," comments Robert H. Mounce. "As God promised Abraham, they are in number as the stars of heaven (Gen. 15:5) and the sand of the sea (Gen. 22:17)."[40] The fourfold division into nations (*ethnē,* as in Matt. 28:19), tribes, peoples, and tongues (language groups) demonstrates the global reach of salvation, and shows that the Abrahamic covenant and the Great Commission have been fulfilled in a magnificent, superabundant way. Here is not merely the cumulation of tiny remnants from each people group, but truly the "full number of the Gentiles" (Rom. 11:25), a multitude

40. Robert H. Mounce, *The Book of Revelation* (Grand Rapids: Eerdmans, 1977), p. 171.

which no man can number! As God's original promises to Abraham stretched his imagination to the breaking point, so does this vision of the ultimate success of God's saving purpose challenge us to not limit our hopes by human assessments of the present progress of Christian missions.

The New Testament sets forth not only the hope for the salvation of the "full number of the Gentiles" but also for the conversion of Israel. In Romans 11:25–26 Paul writes, "Lest you be wise in your own conceits, I want you to understand this mystery, brethren: a hardening has come upon part of Israel, until the full number of the Gentiles come in, and so all Israel will be saved . . . ." This phrase *all Israel (pas Israēl)* has, of course, been subject to a diversity of interpretations. Calvin took it to mean the church (cf. Gal. 6:16, "the Israel of God"). Lenski and others understand it to refer to the cumulated remnant of believing Jews over the centuries.[41]

As F. F. Bruce has pointed out, however, it seems quite artificial to read a meaning for "Israel" in verse 26 different from the sense of "Israel" in verse 25 ("a hardening has come upon part of Israel"). In verse 25 the Israel that is hardened is clearly ethnic Israel, the nation as a whole that has not responded to the gospel. The phrase *all Israel* is a recurring one in Jewish literature, Bruce observes, "where it does not mean 'every Jew without a single exception' but 'Israel as a whole.' Thus 'all Israel has a portion in the age to come,' says the Mishnah tractate *Sanhedrin* (x.i), and proceeds immediately to name those Israelites who have no portion therein."[42] As Franz J. Leenhardt has pointed out, the term *all Israel* forms a contrast with the "remnant" (v. 5); both phrases have clear ethnic con-

---

41. R. C. H. Lenski, *The Interpretation of St. Paul's Epistle to the Romans* (Minneapolis: Augsburg, 1961), p. 727; Charles M. Horne, "The Meaning of the Phrase, 'And Thus All Israel Will Be Saved' (Rom. 11:26)," *Evangelical Theological Society Journal* 21 (1978): 334.

42. F. F. Bruce, *The Epistle of Paul to the Romans* (Grand Rapids: Eerdmans, 1963), pp. 221–22.

notations.[43] Elsewhere in Romans 9–11 the term *Israel* clearly refers to ethnic Israel (9:3–5; 9:6; 9:30–31; 10:19; 10:21; 11:1; 11:7; 11:25).

Paul thus looks forward to a time when the nation of Israel will recognize her true Messiah and enjoy the blessings of salvation in Jesus Christ. No mention is made here, however, of the restoration of an earthly Davidic kingdom, for what Paul envisioned for his people was something infinitely better.[44]

The closing pages of the New Testament contain a marvelous vision of the New Jerusalem in all its vastness and glory:

> And he who talked to me had a measuring rod of gold to measure the city and its gates and walls. The city lies foursquare, its length the same as its breadth; and he measured the city with his rod, twelve thousand stadia; its length and breadth and height are equal. [Rev. 21:15–16]

The church, the New Jerusalem, is depicted as a cube, reminiscent of the Holy of Holies in the tabernacle and the Solomonic temple. The three equal dimensions of the cube are symbolic of spiritual perfection.[45]

Each side of the city is twelve thousand stadia or about fifteen hundred miles long, so that the surface area of the New Jerusalem is some 2,250,000 square miles. In the rabbinic literature there were descriptions of a recreated Jerusalem that would reach Damascus and cover the whole of Palestine, but John's vision dwarfs even those.[46]

The point here is surely that the proportions of the heavenly city, God's church, are incredibly vast. This is consis-

---

43. Franz J. Leenhardt, *The Epistle to the Romans: A Commentary*, trans. Harold Knight (Cleveland: World, 1961), p. 293.

44. Bruce, *The Epistle of Paul to the Romans,* p. 221.

45. R. C. H. Lenski, *The Interpretation of St. John's Revelation* (Minneapolis: Augsburg, 1961), p. 637.

46. William Barclay, *The Revelation of John,* 2 vols. (Philadelphia: Westminster, 1976), vol. 2, p. 212.

tent with the reference to the "countless multitude" (Rev.
7:9). The ultimate outcome of the church's missionary
efforts will far surpass our current human expectations,
because God "by the power at work within us is able to do
far more abundantly than all that we ask or think" (Eph.
3:20). The New Testament's witness to the final greatness
of the kingdom is a constant source of encouragement to
the church in its mission. Believing these things, God's
people can be "steadfast, immovable, always abounding in
the work of the Lord, knowing that in the Lord your labor
is not in vain" (1 Cor. 15:58).

4

The Growth of the Kingdom in History

"The kingdom of God . . . is like a grain of mustard seed, which, when sown upon the ground, is the smallest of all the seeds . . . ; yet when it is sown it grows up and becomes the greatest of all shrubs. . . ." [Mark 4:30–32]

"During the 20th century . . . Christianity has become the most extensive and universal religion in history," observed David B. Barrett, editor of the massive *World Christian Encyclopedia,* the definitive work on the current status of Christianity around the globe. "There are today Christians and organized Christian churches in every inhabited country on earth. The church is therefore now, for the first time in history, ecumenical in the literal meaning of the word: its boundaries are coextensive with the *oikumenē,* the whole inhabited world."[1]

---

1. David B. Barrett, ed., *World Christian Encyclopedia* (Nairobi: Oxford University Press, 1982), p. 3.

The history of the expansion of the Christian church can
be seen as a series of nine major pulsations or epochs, five
of which were times of advance and four of which were
times of retreat.[2] "Each major period of crisis and decline
is followed by another of advance," wrote Kenneth Scott
Latourette, the noted historian of missions. "When mankind is seen as a whole, the influence of Christianity upon
it becomes, in the course of these pulsations, progressively
more extensive."[3]

The "mustard seed" of the kingdom of Christ has indeed
grown in a dramatic way from its very humble and insignificant beginnings nineteen centuries ago. This chapter
will review some of the highlights of the history of the
expansion of Christianity, in order to encourage faith in
the growth and ultimate victory of God's kingdom, and to
glean insights for the church's ongoing missionary task.

The Early Church Wins the Roman Empire

"One of the most amazing and significant facts of history," notes Latourette, "is that within five centuries of its
birth Christianity won the professed allegiance of the
overwhelming majority of the population of the Roman
Empire and even the support of the Roman state."[4] How in
fact did this remarkable turn of events come about?

Prior to the reign of Constantine (306–37) Christianity
spread in the Roman Empire without official sanction and
often against considerable opposition. The "most rapid expansion of the new movement took place in Asia Minor,
where Paul's missionary outreach to a strongly Hellenis-
tic populace was preeminently successful."[5] The native

---

2. Ibid.

3. Kenneth Scott Latourette, *The Christian Outlook* (New York: Harper and
Row, 1948), p. 42.

4. Kenneth Scott Latourette, *A History of Christianity* (London: Eyre and
Spottiswoode, n.d.), p. 65.

5. Robert J. Torbet, "Expansion of Christianity (Ancient)," *Twentieth Century Encyclopedia of Religious Knowledge,* ed. Lefferts A. Loetscher (Grand
Rapids: Baker, 1955), p. 411.

cultures and religious cults were in a state of decline, and the many Gentile proselytes to Judaism provided a natural point of contact for the apostle's evangelistic endeavors. Paul's preaching in the synagogues and in public places led to the gathering of house churches in the various cities which were the focus of his mission. Paul's basic mission strategy, in fact, relied significantly on establishing a Christian fellowship in a household of some size and from there working out into others in the town. The Christian community at Corinth, for example, seemed to be made up of a number of house churches. Paul baptized the households of Crispus, Gaius, and Stephanas, all of some social standing (1 Cor. 1:14–16).[6] These early house churches had the merit of integrating Christian faith into the context of the people's daily lives, rather than merely into an institutional setting.

By 306, Christianity was still a minority religion in Greece. In Egypt and in and around Carthage it was quite strong by the end of the second century. The church was fairly firmly established in southern Spain by the early part of the third century, and by the middle of the third century, Italy appears to have had about one hundred bishoprics. The presence of the church in the Rhone Valley is indicated by persecutions in Lyons and Vienne in 177. The gospel had been carried to Gaul and possibly also to Britain by the end of the second century or earlier.[7]

The church was expanding eastward as well. By 225 twenty Christian bishoprics were established in the Tigris-Euphrates Valley and on the borders of Persia. By the beginning of the third century Christianity had secured a foothold in Armenia, and "the Goths, to the north and west of the Black Sea, [had] received the Faith from captives taken in A.D. 258 from Cappadocian Christians."

---

6. Rafael Aguirre, "Early Christian House Churches," *Theology Digest* 32:2 (1985): 152.

7. Torbet, "Expansion of Christianity (Ancient)," p. 411.

Ulfilas, who worked from about 341 to 380, was a notable
missionary to the Goths north of the Danube. Christianity
may have arrived in India before the end of the third century from Alexandria and merchants to the East.[8]

It is noteworthy that the early church had its greatest
success in the large urban areas of the empire. "The early
missionaries moved from city to city and rapidly spread
the gospel over a very wide area," notes A. H. M. Jones.
"The early churches were thus urban communities, and
they tended to remain so."[9] Given the fact that world population growth for the foreseeable future will be concentrated in the cities, this success of the early church in
urban areas should be an encouragement to the missionary efforts of the present.

The writings of the church fathers indicate that within
three centuries Christianity had penetrated nearly every
level of society. The church was attractive to the poor and
dispossessed, but appealed to other classes as well. At the
beginning of the second century, Pliny, the Roman gover-
nor of the province of Bythinia in Asia Minor, complained
to the emperor Trajan that people of every age, rank, and
sex had forsaken the temples to follow the Christian way.
Tertullian, writing about a century later, could say to the
heathen with very little exaggeration, "We are but of yes-
terday, and yet we already fill your cities, islands, camps,
your palace, senate and forum; we have left to you only
your temples."[10]

According to Adolf Harnack, half of the population in
Asia Minor, Thrace, and Armenia were professing Chris-
tians by 325. In Syria, Egypt, Greece, Macedonia, central
North Africa, Spain, Rome, and southern Italy, Chris-

8. Ibid., pp. 411–12.
9. A. H. M. Jones, "The Social Background of the Struggle between Paganism and Christianity," in *The Conflict Between Paganism and Christianity in
the Fourth Century,* ed. Arnaldo Momigliano (London: Oxford University
Press, 1963), p. 18.
10. Cited by Torbet, "Expansion of Christianity (Ancient)," p. 412.

tianity was becoming the predominant religion.[11] The historian Ramsay MacMullen has estimated that Christianity was winning new converts on the order of five hundred thousand in each generation from the end of the first century to 313, the year of Constantine's edict of toleration. "No other new cult anywhere nearly approached the same success," he observed.[12]

What were the reasons for this remarkable growth? Latourette has pointed to at least nine different factors which contributed to this dynamic expansion of the church.[13] The conversion of the emperor Constantine and his endorsement of the Christian religion gave further impetus to trends already under way. It meant as well, however, that many half-converted people were now entering the church, with a consequent slackening of spiritual fervor and discipline.

The disintegration of Greco-Roman society opened doors for the Christian faith. The church offered security and fellowship in an uncertain and increasingly impersonal world. Christianity offered a sense of community, tangible human warmth, and a basis for self-worth and meaning to its adherents. "Christians were in a more than formal sense 'members of one another,'" observed classical scholar E. R. Dodds. "I think that was a major cause, perhaps the strongest single cause, of the spread of Christianity."[14] This attractive power of authentic Christian fellowship and community in the early church is of enduring significance for the church's mission today.

---

11. Adolf Harnack, *The Mission and Expansion of Christianity in the First Three Centuries,* cited by Torbet, "Expansion of Christianity (Ancient)," p. 412.

12. Ramsay MacMullen, *Christianizing the Roman Empire: A.D. 100–400* (New Haven: Yale University Press, 1984), p. 110.

13. Kenneth Scott Latourette, *History of the Expansion of Christianity,* vol. 1, *The First Five Centuries* (New York: Harper and Brothers, 1937), pp. 162ff.

14. E. R. Dodds, *Pagan and Christian in an Age of Anxiety: Some Aspects of Religious Experience from Marcus Aurelius to Constantine* (Cambridge: Cambridge University Press, 1965), p. 138.

The church's organizational strength also contributed to its success. "No one of its rivals possessed so powerful and coherent a structure as did the church," wrote Latourette. "No other gave to its adherents quite the same feeling of coming into a closely knit community."[15] The Christian community was characterized by a sense of inclusiveness. It attracted adherents from all classes and races more successfully than any of its competitors.[16]

The early church was also successful because it could be flexible in adapting to new cultural conditions, but at the same time was uncompromising in its most fundamental beliefs. Christianity was tough-minded in its insistence that salvation is to be found in Christ alone. As Michael Green has noted, the early Christians "really believed that men without Christ might suffer eternal and irreparable loss, and this thought drove them to unremitting labors to reach them with the gospel. There was no hint of universalism in the early Church. . . ."[17] In a similar vein MacMullen has observed that the early church's sense of urgency, zeal for evangelism, and "the demand that the believer deny the title of god to all but one, made up the force that alternative beliefs could not match."[18] Christianity's sociological inclusivity and theological exclusivity formed a potent combination unmatched by its rivals.

Christianity answered the ancient world's longing for immortality and union with God. Its connection with Judaism lent it the prestige of an ancient religious tradition.[19] Its religious and theological insights were concretized in the "driving power of personality" in the story of the life, death, and resurrection of Jesus of Nazareth.[20]

---

15. Latourette, *The First Five Centuries,* p. 164.
16. Ibid.
17. Michael Green, *Evangelism in the Early Church* (London: Hodder and Stoughton, 1970), p. 275.
18. MacMullen, *Christianizing the Roman Empire,* p. 110.
19. Latourette, *The First Five Centuries,* pp. 165–66.
20. S. Angus, *The Environment of Early Christianity* (London: Duckworth, 1914), p. 265.

The high moral standards of the church and its demonstrated compassion for the less fortunate were important features of its life that attracted outsiders. Christianity set forth lofty ethical ideals and at the same time could demonstrate the power of those ideals to transform the lives of individuals. In pagan religions, on the other hand, "the morality of the gods was lower than that of their worshippers," noted S. Angus. "The gods were gradually improved by their worshippers, but not *vice versa*."[21] Christians demonstrated love for their fellow men and women by caring for widows and orphans, helping the sick, infirm, and disabled, reaching out to slaves, prisoners, and those languishing in the mines, helping to find work for the unemployed, assisting in time of natural disasters, and showing hospitality to strangers and travelers.[22] These acts of benevolence and compassion were in themselves powerful forms of evangelism.

Less well known today is the fact that the demonstrated ability of early Christians to exorcise demons constituted a powerful weapon in their evangelistic arsenal. Tertullian is only one of many Christian Fathers who could confidently speak to pagans about the spiritual power demonstrated by the followers of the resurrected Christ: "Were it not for us, who would free you from those hidden foes that are ever making havoc of your health in soul and body—from those raids of the demons, I mean, which we repel from you without reward or desire . . . We do more than repudiate the demons: we overcome them, we expose them daily to contempt, and exorcise them from their victims, as well known to many people."[23]

"The manhandling of demons—humiliating them, making them howl, beg for mercy, tell their secrets, and depart in a hurry—served a purpose quite essential to the

---

21. Ibid., p. 60.
22. Harnack, *The Mission and Expansion of Christianity,* trans. James Moffatt, 2 vols. (London: Williams and Norgate, n.d.), vol. 1, p. 153.
23. Ibid., p. 141.

Christian definition of monotheism," noted MacMullen. "It made physically (or dramatically) visible the superiority of the Christian's patron Power over all others."[24] In a way reminiscent of Elijah's contest with the priests of Baal (1 Kings 18), the God of the Christians could demonstrate his reality by "answering by fire." The ability of the early Christians to exorcise demons showed that the "kingdom of God does not consist in talk but in power" (1 Cor. 4:20), and the point was not lost on the pagans. The importance of such head-on "power encounters" with spiritual opponents needs to be recovered in the church's mission today.

Behind all these factors in the church's expansion was the dynamic presence of the risen Christ himself in the midst of his people. Jesus was not merely an ethical teacher from the past, but the living and powerful Lord in the spiritual experience of believers. "Without Jesus," Latourette observes, "Christianity would not have sprung into existence, and from him and beliefs about him came its main dynamic."[25] The spiritual vitality energized the laity to share their faith with their neighbors. "The spontaneous outreach of the total Christian community," writes Green, "gave immense impetus to the movement from the very outset."[26]

The Middle Ages: Advances and Declines

The history of the spread of Christianity during the Middle Ages presents a mixed picture; there were both significant advances and declines. On the negative side, the explosive growth of Islam in the seventh and later centuries meant territorial losses for Christianity in the Middle East and North Africa that have yet to be regained.

24. MacMullen, *Christianizing the Roman Empire*, p. 28.
25. Latourette, *The First Five Centuries*, p. 168.
26. Green, *Evangelism in the Early Church*, p. 274.

After only three centuries Islam was almost as geographically widespread as the Christian faith.[27]

The successive waves of invasions by the barbarians and the Vikings created social upheavals in the dying Roman Empire, and by 950 the cultural attainments of Christianity were probably lower than what they had been in the fourth and fifth centuries. Because of cultural, political, and theological differences, the Western and Eastern branches of the Christian church were also drifting apart during this period.

On the other hand, significant signs of missionary and cultural creativity were not lacking during this period. With the increasing worldliness in the church after the conversion of Constantine, there was also the rise of the monastic movement, which attempted to maintain the rigor and spirituality of the earlier Christian vision. It was in fact the monasteries that provided the leadership for the church's missionary efforts during these centuries subsequent to the decline of the old Roman state.

Monks such as Saint Patrick (c. 389–c. 461) carried Christianity to Ireland, and Celtic missionaries brought the gospel to Scotland, where Saint Columba established the monastery at Iona in the sixth century. Columbanus (d. 615) led evangelistic missions in France and the Rhineland. Wilfred and Boniface (d. 755) did notable work among the Germanic and Scandinavian tribes of pagan Europe. Many people of Polish and Magyar stock were converted through the work of Saint Stephen in the tenth century, and the baptism of Vladimir of Kiev (c. 988) brought many Russians into the Orthodox faith.[28]

The collapsing social order of the Roman Empire was

---

27. Latourette, *A History of Christianity*, p. 275.

28. "Missions," *Oxford Dictionary of the Christian Church*, ed. F. L. Cross and E. A. Livingstone (Oxford: Oxford University Press, 1974), pp. 922–23, and "Missions, Christian," Ian Breward, *New International Dictionary of the Christian Church*, ed. J. D. Douglas (Grand Rapids: Zondervan, 1974), pp. 664–65.

not a purely negative factor in the life of the church during
this period. It did, to be sure, mean a great deal of social
dislocation and confusion, but at the same time it gave
the church the opportunity to demonstrate the strength
of its own leadership and organization. The energetic
missionary monks such as Saint Boniface brought organizational skills, educational resources, and new farming
methods which were not readily available from other
sources.[29] The collapse of the old social order in fact freed
Christianity from the restrictions placed on it by its close
association with the Roman state and gave greater opportunity for its inherent genius to express itself. Christianity showed more vigor and creativity in the West than
in the East, where the church remained tied to and subser-
vient to the rather static cultural and political structures
of the Byzantine Empire. It was from the Western church,
rather than the Eastern, that the great bursts of missionary energy in later centuries were to come. One of Augustine's key insights in *The City of God* was that the fate
of the church was not tied to the temporal fortunes of the
city of Rome and the empire it represented. Christianity's
ability to "disenculturate" itself meant that times of social
decline and turmoil were not necessarily disastrous for the
church, but rather opportunities to demonstrate new vitality and creativity in its missionary advance.

The Age of Discovery and Conquest: Roman Catholic Missions

The age of European colonial expansion was also the
period when Roman Catholicism was brought to the

---

29. William Carroll Bark, *Origins of the Medieval World* (Stanford: Stanford
University Press, 1958), p. 79. Bark shows that the early medieval period was
not a period of unrelieved "darkness," but a period when significant tech-
nological advances were made: the wheeled plow, the water mill, the horse
collar, the crank, and other devices which were sources of greater material
productivity.

Americas and to Asia. In 1493 Pope Alexander VI divided the non-Christian lands between Spain and Portugal, the two dominant world powers at the time. All the Americas except Brazil fell to Spain. The conquistadores imposed Spanish civilization and Roman Catholicism by force, at times treating the natives with considerable cruelty. Some missionaries such as Bartholome de las Casas, however, struggled courageously to obtain more just and humane treatment for the natives.

Catholic orders such as the Dominicans, the Franciscans, and the Augustinians did notable missionary work during this period. The newly formed Jesuit order, under the leadership of Francis Xavier (d. 1552), took the Christian faith to India, Malaya, and Japan. Other Jesuit missionaries worked in Japan and China, and Matteo Ricci and his successors experimented with adapting Christianity to Chinese culture. These experiments in "contextualization" of the gospel had some initial success, but because of political changes and dissension between various Catholic mission orders and restrictive policies by the Roman hierarchy, Christianity had virtually died out in Japan by 1650 and in China by 1723. The decline of Spain and Portugal and the rise of the Protestant European powers brought this particular period of Roman Catholic expansion to an end.[30]

Because of the political conditions in Europe and the religious climate the eighteenth century saw little in the way of vigorous missionary activity. In the nineteenth century, however, Roman Catholic missions experienced a strong revival. The Society for the Propagation of the Faith was founded in 1822, and new missionary orders such as the Marists were established to take advantage of French colonial expansion in Indochina, Africa, and the Pacific. Missionary leaders such as Cardinal Lavigerie

---

30. "Missions," *Westminster Dictionary of Church History,* ed. Jerald C. Brauer (Philadelphia: Westminster, 1971), p. 558.

(d. 1892) spoke out strongly against slavery and contributed much to African education and technical advancement. Roman Catholic missions were especially strong in
educational and charitable work, and women's religious
orders also played an active role in this period. According
to some estimates there were more than eight million converts to Catholicism from paganism during the nineteenth century.[31]

In retrospect this period of Roman Catholic missionary
expansion represents a mixed picture. Christianity did
spread far beyond the borders of Europe and the Mediter-
ranean basin as a result, but at the cost of being inextrica-
bly associated with Western colonialism in the minds of
the subject peoples. This same problem of disentangling
the essentials of Christian faith from its Western political
and cultural trappings was also to face Protestant missionaries in succeeding centuries.

Modern Protestant Missions

Protestant churches displayed little interest in missions during the Reformation, being preoccupied with internal reforms and the struggles with Roman Catholicism. The rediscovery of the heart of the gospel message,
the stress on the calling of all believers to serve Christ, the
new interest in the Bible, and the concern for a literate
laity, however, all laid important foundations for later
Protestant missionary efforts.

The first Protestant missionary society, the Society for
the Propagation of the Gospel in New England, was established in England in 1649. The Mayhews and John Eliot
began the work of evangelizing the Indian tribes in New
England during the 1640s.

The seventeenth century also witnessed extensive ac-

---

31. James De Jong, "Expansion World-Wide," *Eerdmans' Handbook to
Christian History,* ed. Tim Dowley (Grand Rapids: Eerdmans, 1977), p. 476.

tivity by the chaplains of the Dutch East India trading company. By the middle of the next century there were well over three hundred thousand Protestants in Sri Lanka (Ceylon) as a result of these efforts.

The German Pietism of Philip Jacob Spener (1635–1705) and August Hermann Francke (1663–1727) contributed significantly to the rise of Protestant missions. Francke trained missionaries at Halle and the Danish king Frederick IV sent them to Tranquebar in southern India, beginning in 1705.

The Moravians, under the leadership of Count Nicholas von Zinzendorf, were important pioneers in the modern missionary movement. Despite the group's small size, it sent out hundreds of its own missionaries and inspired many others. By 1740 Moravian missionaries had reached the Virgin Islands, Greenland, Surinam, the Gold Coast, North America, and South Africa. "Their self-sacrifice, love and total commitment to evangelization," James De Jong has observed, "are unparalleled in the history of missions." The Moravians pointed forward to the nineteenth and twentieth centuries, when missions would come to be regarded as the duty of every denomination.

The evangelical awakenings of the eighteenth century, fostered by the labors of John and Charles Wesley, George Whitefield, Jonathan Edwards, and others, gave tremendous impetus to the development of the missionary movement. The Baptist Missionary Society was founded by William Carey in 1792, the London Missionary Society in 1795, and the Church Missionary Society in 1799. American missionary societies began to organize in 1787, and a student movement at Williams College and Andover Seminary led to the founding of the American Board of Commissioners for Foreign Missions in 1810.

Carey's 1792 book, *An Enquiry into the Obligation of Christians to Use Means for the Conversion of the Heathen*, is a landmark in the history of Protestant missions. Carey awakened the churches to their missionary respon-

sibilities, arguing that the Great Commission still applied
to all believers, not just to the first generation of apostles.[32] Over against a form of hyper-Calvinism that argued, in effect, "If God wants to save the elect, he can do so
without our help," Carey pointed out that God accom-
plishes his sovereign ends through the use of responsible
human means, that is, missionaries. Carey is also remem-
bered for his famous slogan, "Expect great things from
God; attempt great things for God"—a motto that he himself energetically exemplified in a long career of missionary service in India.

Latourette has called the nineteenth century the "great
century" of Christian missions. The period from 1815 to
1914 witnessed the greatest numerical and geographical
expansion of the missionary enterprise of any epoch up
until that time. A great burst of activity by missionary
agencies, Bible societies, and denominations made Christianity a truly worldwide faith.

The founding of the China Inland Mission in 1865 by
J. Hudson Taylor marked the first of many "faith missions," independent of denominational control and supported entirely by voluntary contributions. The independent faith missions continue to be a central feature of
Protestant evangelical missions today.

Protestant missionaries worked diligently in Africa,
Asia, and Oceania. At times the missionaries were not
successful in separating the gospel from its Western colonial form, as witnessed by the Boxer Rebellion in China
(1900) and the Nyasaland Rising (1915) in Africa, which
demonstrated the depth of native resentment at the confusion of colonialism and Christianity.

These problems should not obscure the fact, however,
that Protestant missionaries in the nineteenth century
made tremendous spiritual and cultural contributions to

---

32. A. F. Walls, "Outposts of Empire," *Eerdmans' Handbook to Christian History,* p. 548.

the lands in which they worked. Missionaries were active in the fight against slavery. Medical services and education were hallmarks of the missionary presence. Notable contributions were made by missionaries in the areas of linguistics, ethnography, and comparative religion. Cannibalism and infanticide were checked, and new respect for the dignity of women was taught. The introduction of new products like cocoa into Ghana (1857), together with new farming methods, dramatically improved native economies. Countless lives were transformed by the power of the gospel and vigorous churches established. Missionary statesmen such as Rufus Anderson (d. 1880) and Henry Venn vigorously promoted the formation of national churches that would not be mere dependents of Western ones, but which would be "self-governing, self-supporting, and self-propagating."[33]

During the course of the nineteenth century virtually every Protestant denomination became actively involved in the task of foreign missions. By 1910 there were about 420 direct sending agencies.[34]

Looking back over this remarkable period as a whole, Latourette has noted that the Christian faith came to the year 1914 "on a rising tide and with mounting momentum." In spite of adversaries and some setbacks, by 1914 "it was more widely spread geographically than at any previous time, it had given rise to men and movements which were as astounding as any in the history of the faith, and it was making its impress upon more of mankind than ever before."[35] The "mustard seed" was indeed demonstrating remarkable growth.

The Twentieth Century

"We are in the springtime of Christian missions," stated church-growth expert C. Peter Wagner. "The last couple of

---

33. "Missions," *Westminster Dictionary of Church History,* p. 559.
34. Ibid.
35. Latourette, *A History of Christianity,* p. 1345.

decades of the twentieth century hold forth more promise for the dynamic spread of the Christian faith around the globe than any other period of time since Jesus turned the water into wine."[36]

Recent trends in missionary activity and church growth around the world would appear to support this optimistic outlook. The total number of North American Protestant missionaries working overseas rose from 34,460 in 1969 to 53,494 in 1979, an increase of more than 50 percent in ten years.[37] Today there are more than 450 North American Protestant mission sending agencies, 300 of which are independent and nonaffiliated.[38]

Each day an estimated seventy-eight thousand new Christians are added to the church around the world as a result of both biological and conversion growth. One result of this dramatic growth is that every week approximately one thousand new churches are established in Asia and Africa alone. Many of these are small, struggling groups meeting in a home or school, but nevertheless represent committed gatherings of believers.[39] Bible translation has made tremendous progress in the twentieth century, with Scriptures available in more than seventeen hundred languages, covering 97 percent of the world's population.

On the other hand, membership in Christian churches in Europe, North America, and Communist nations has declined markedly in the twentieth century, in striking contrast to the growth in the Third World.[40] Much of this decline has occurred among merely nominal adherents to

---

36. C. Peter Wagner, "The Greatest Church Growth Is Beyond Our Shores," *Christianity Today* 28:8 (1984): 25.

37. Ibid.

38. Robert T. Coote, "The Uneven Growth of Conservative Evangelical Missions," *International Bulletin of Missionary Research* 6:3 (1982): 118–23.

39. C. Peter Wagner, *On the Crest of the Wave: Becoming a World Christian* (Ventura, Calif.: Regal, 1983), excerpted in *Mission Frontiers*, August-September 1983, pp. 21–28. Much of the following information on church growth is from this source.

40. Barrett, *World Christian Encyclopedia*, p. 7.

Christianity, but the inroads made by secularism and materialism are disturbing nonetheless.

In much of the developing world the picture is quite different. In parts of Latin America the Protestant churches are growing three times faster than the rate of population growth. In 1900 only fifty thousand Protestants were counted in Latin America, but by 1980 the figure was more than twenty million. Some estimate that by the year 2000 there will be one hundred million Protestants in Latin America. Much of the most dramatic growth has been among the Pentecostal churches. In Guatemala, for example, the Assemblies of God churches have been growing at a rate of 44 percent per year.[41]

Church growth in Africa has been even more dramatic than that in Latin America. According to Barrett, the most massive influx into the Christian church in history has been taking place in Africa during the last one hundred years. In 1900 there were fewer than ten million African Christians. Now there are more than two hundred million, and four hundred million have been projected by the year 2000. "This means," notes Wagner, "that Christians will have grown from nine percent of the African population to 48 percent in our century."[42]

Korea has been a "flash point" of church growth in the twentieth century. One hundred years ago there were no churches in Korea; now there are six thousand in the city of Seoul alone. The world's largest congregation is the Yoido Full Gospel Church in Seoul, pastored by Paul Yonggi Cho, with more than 270,000 members divided into nineteen thousand home cell groups. Six new churches are being started in South Korea every day.[43]

The growth of the church in China has been one of the great surprises of the century. When the missionaries

41. Wagner, *On the Crest of the Wave*, pp. 24–25.
42. Ibid., p. 25.
43. Ibid., p. 26.

were expelled in 1949–50 by the Communist government, the prospects for Christianity did not look bright. In 1949 Protestant churches counted some 840,000 communicant members. According to Jonathan Chao of the Chinese Church Research Center in Hong Kong, there are now between thirty-five and fifty million believers in China, most of whom meet in small house churches. This amounts to a growth of at least thirty-five- to fifty-fold during the period 1949–83.[44] These remarkable figures are a testimony to the power of the Holy Spirit and the Word of God to cause Christ's kingdom in China to grow despite great obstacles and beyond all normal human expectations.

In retrospect, then, it would seem that the twentieth century is seeing striking confirmations of the growth of Christ's kingdom promised in the Old and New Testaments. "In Jesus' day," observes Barrett, "the rapid growth of a mustard seed startled his followers; in the same way today, the vast expansion of the influence of the Kingdom of God exceeds all the expectations of earlier generations of Christians."[45]

In 1948 Latourette wrote that far from dying out, "Christianity, so history leads us confidently to predict, is in its youth and is to continue to mount as a factor in the human scene."[46] That hopeful outlook has indeed been confirmed by the remarkable expansion of Christ's church in the latter part of the twentieth century.

---

44. Jonathan Chao, "The Structure of House Churches," *China and the Church Today*, March-April 1983, p. 8.

45. Barrett, *World Christian Encyclopedia*, p. 19.

46. Latourette, *The Christian Outlook*, p. 194.

5

Revelation 20:1–6

Then I saw an angel coming down from heaven, holding in his hand the key of the bottomless pit and a great chain. And he seized the dragon, that ancient serpent, who is the Devil and Satan, and bound him for a thousand years, and threw him into the pit, and shut it and sealed it over him, that he should deceive the nations no more, till the thousand years were ended. After that he must be loosed for a little while.

Then I saw thrones, and seated on them were those to whom judgment was committed. Also I saw the souls of those who had been beheaded for their testimony to Jesus and for the word of God, and who had not worshiped the beast or its image and had not received its mark on their foreheads or their hands. They came to life, and reigned with Christ a thousand years. The rest of the dead did not come to life until the thousand years were ended. This is the first resurrection. Blessed and holy is he who shares in the first resurrection! Over such the second death has no power, but they shall be priests of God and of Christ, and they shall reign with him a thousand years.

The New Testament scholar Leon Morris has commented that students of Scripture need to approach the twentieth chapter of the Book of Revelation with "humility and charity."[1] It is obvious that Revelation 20:1–6 has great relevance for any discussion of the millennial question, but at the same time it is clear that conservative interpreters have not been able to achieve consensus about the meaning of this passage.

What is the relationship between the literal and the metaphorical elements in this text and in the Book of Revelation generally? Is there a clear chronological connection between chapters 19 and 20? Is the second coming of Christ described in 19:11–21, and presupposed in 20:1–6? When exactly is Satan bound (v. 2)? Did this occur in some sense during the earthly ministry of Jesus, or is it a wholly future event? What is the exact force of the statement about Satan's deceiving the nations (vv. 3, 8)? Is the expression *a thousand years* (vv. 2, 4–6) literal or symbolic of a long period of time? Where are the thrones (v. 4) located—in heaven or on earth? What is the significance of the fact that John refers to "souls" (v. 4) but not bodies? And perhaps most crucially, do the terms *they came to life* and *first resurrection* (vv. 4–5) refer to bodily resurrection, or are they metaphorical expressions for a spiritual reality? These are some of the important exegetical questions that need to be addressed in an attempt to assess the bearing of Revelation 20:1–6 on the general postmillennial framework developed on the basis of other Old and New Testament passages.

For the purposes of this discussion some of the major arguments of the premillennial and amillennial interpretations of this passage will first be presented. An attempt will then be made to bring together valid insights from both these positions, and to show how Revelation

---

1. Leon Morris, *The Revelation of St. John: An Introduction and Commentary* (Grand Rapids: Eerdmans, 1969), p. 233.

20:1–6 can be understood within the general outlines of
the postmillennial framework.

Premillennial Interpretation

The term *premillennial* refers to the position which
holds that Christ returns physically to earth prior (hence
"pre") to the millennial reign described in Revelation
20:4–6. The text is understood in terms of a "first resurrection" which is bodily, and the saints reign with Christ
for a thousand years on earth. This type of interpretation
was held in the early church by Papias, Barnabas,
Irenaeus, Justin Martyr, and Tertullian,[2] and today is advocated in various forms by evangelical scholars such as
George E. Ladd, John F. Walvoord, G. R. Beasley-Murray,
and Robert H. Mounce.[3]

Premillennial interpreters generally hold that 19:11–21
describes the second coming of Christ, and that there is a
clear chronological connection between chapters 19 and
20. Consequently, Christ is understood to be present on
earth while the events of 20:1–6 are taking place.

The binding of Satan is held to be a future event. Although Satan may have been bound in some sense during
Christ's earthly ministry (Matt. 12:29; John 12:31; Col.

---

2. Hans Bietenhard, "The Millennial Hope in the Early Church," *Scottish
Journal of Theology* 6 (1953): 12–30. C. Mazzucco and E. Pietrella, "Il rapporto
tra la concezione del millennio dei primi autori cristiani e l' *Apocalisse* de
Giovanni," *Augustinianum* 18 (1978): 29–45, cited in *New Testament Abstracts*
23 (1979): 55, argue that the premillennialism of Justin and Irenaeus is more
indebted to Jewish apocalyptic sources and Jewish-Christian tradition than to
the text of Revelation.

3. On the premillennial interpretation, see George E. Ladd, *A Commentary
on the Revelation of John* (Grand Rapids: Eerdmans, 1972); G. R. Beasley-
Murray, *The Book of Revelation* (Grand Rapids: Eerdmans, 1974); John F.
Walvoord, *The Revelation of Jesus Christ: A Commentary* (Chicago: Moody,
1966); Robert H. Mounce, *The Book of Revelation* (Grand Rapids: Eerdmans,
1977); Jack S. Deere, "Premillennialism in Rev. 20:4–6," *Bibliotheca Sacra* 135
(1978): 58–73; J. R. Michaels, "The First Resurrection: A Response," *Westminster Theological Journal* 39 (1976): 100–109.

2:15), it is argued that other texts which refer to the present activity of Satan (Eph. 2:2; especially 1 Peter 5:8,
"Your adversary the devil prowls around like a roaring
lion, seeking some one to devour") clearly indicate that a
more total restriction of Satan's activity is still to be expected. The continuing existence and influence of false
religions show that Satan is still deceiving the nations
(v. 3) in the present age.

The "thousand years" can be understood as a literal
thousand-year reign of Christ with the saints on earth.
Although there are certainly symbolic uses of numbers in
Revelation, there seem to be no compelling reasons in the
immediate context that demand a nonliteral understanding of the thousand years.[4]

The thrones (v. 4) are understood to be located on earth.
Revelation 5:10 is adduced in support, where it is stated of
the redeemed that "they shall reign on earth." Also cited
in this connection is Matthew 19:28, where Christ tells his
disciples that in the new age "you who have followed me
will also sit on twelve thrones, judging the twelve tribes of
Israel."

The noun *souls* (v. 4) refers to whole persons, rather
than to disembodied spirits in heaven. It is noted that the
souls under the altar (6:9) are said to be given a white robe
(6:11), implying that they have bodily form. In 18:13, in a
chapter describing the doom of Babylon, John refers to
slaves as "human souls."

The phrase *they came to life* (*ezēsan*, v. 4), which refers
to the "first resurrection," is taken to mean a bodily resurrection of the martyrs (and perhaps others) at the beginning of the millennium. This same term *(ezēsan)* is used in
2:8 of the resurrection of Jesus, which certainly was
bodily. Ladd argues that there is no contextual reason in

---

4. Deere, "Premillennialism in Rev. 20:4–6." Ladd, *A Commentary on the
Revelation of John,* p. 262, while holding a premillennial view, admits that the
number one thousand may well be symbolic.

the passage to take *ezēsan* in a physical sense in verse 5
("the rest of the dead did not come to life until the thousand years were ended") and in a metaphorical sense in
verse 4. If the second resurrection is bodily, so must be the
first.[5]

The theological significance of the millennium is to be
found both in the vindication of Christ's lordship within
history and in the demonstration of the justice of God's
ultimate judgment at the end of history. If some still rebel
against the divine order after a thousand-year personal
reign of Christ (20:7–8), when God's truth and goodness
are visibly manifested, then the condemnation of the apos-
tate is shown to be unquestionably just. And as Ladd argues, the final apostasy after the millennial blessings
"makes it plain that the ultimate root of sin is not poverty
or inadequate social conditions or an unfortunate environment; it is the rebelliousness of the human heart."[6]

Amillennial Interpretation

The term *amillennial* refers to an understanding of
Revelation 20:4–6 in which there is no literal thousand-
year reign of Christ with the saints on earth. In this nonliteral approach the expression *thousand years* is generally understood to refer to the entire church age, the
period extending from the resurrection and ascension of
Christ until the second coming. The "first resurrection" is
either Christian conversion or the soul's presence with
Christ in heaven during the period between the individual's death and the final resurrection. In the amillennial
understanding, the second coming of Christ, the resurrection of both the righteous and the wicked, and the last
judgment are essentially simultaneous events.

This approach to Revelation 20:4–6 first became influ-

---

5. Ladd, *A Commentary on the Revelation of John,* p. 266.
6. Ibid., p. 269.

ential through the teaching of Augustine, was later advocated by Martin Luther and the Protestant Reformers, and today is held by scholars such as Morris, R. C. H. Lenski, M. G. Kline, Henry Barclay Swete, and William Hendriksen.[7]

Amillennial interpreters argue that Revelation 20:4–6 must be understood in the context of the apocalyptic and highly visionary style of the book as a whole. In some passages, for example, 1:12–16, the symbolic nature of the language is particularly obvious. When it is said that a "sharp two-edged sword" issues from the mouth of the risen Christ (1:16), it seems clear that this is intended to represent the powerful authority of Christ's spoken word (cf. Eph. 6:17, "the sword of the Spirit, which is the word of God"). In 20:1–3, it is pointed out that the chain (v. 1) is clearly symbolic of God's authority to bind the forces of evil, since Satan, being a spirit, cannot be bound with a literal physical chain. Likewise, the terms *dragon* and *serpent* (v. 2) are figures for the incorporeal adversary of God and his people. Given such manifestly symbolic elements in 20:1–3, and throughout the Apocalypse, why, asks the amillennial interpreter, is it necessary to insist on literal interpretation in 20:4–6?

With respect to the relationship of chapters 19 and 20, 19:11–21 could be taken to refer to the progressive triumph of the risen Christ in heaven over the forces of evil prior to the parousia (cf. 1 Cor. 15:24b–25), while

---

7. For the amillennial approach, see Morris, *The Revelation of St. John;* R. C. H. Lenski, *The Interpretation of St. John's Revelation* (Minneapolis: Augsburg, 1961); Henry Barclay Swete, *Commentary on the Apocalypse of St. John* (Grand Rapids: Eerdmans, 1951); William Hendriksen, *More than Conquerors* (Grand Rapids: Baker, 1939); M. G. Kline, "The First Resurrection," *Westminster Theological Journal* 37 (1975): 366–75; J. A. Hughes, "Revelation 20:4–6 and the Question of the Millennium," *Westminster Theological Journal* 35 (1973): 281–302; N. Shepherd, "The Resurrections of Revelation 20," *Westminster Theological Journal* 37 (1974): 34–43; Sydney H. T. Page, "Revelation 20 and Pauline Eschatology," *Journal of the Evangelical Theological Society* 23:1 (1980): 31–43.

20:11–15, referring to the last judgment, implies the presence of Christ on earth. The phrase *I saw heaven opened* (19:11) recalls Acts 7:56, where Stephen, immediately prior to his martyrdom, says, "I see the heavens opened, and the Son of man standing at the right hand of God." In both cases the vision of "heaven opened" gives those on earth who are facing martyrdom the encouragement that the exalted Christ in heaven reigns victorious over his foes, contrary to all human appearances. The "opening of the heavens" allows the embattled church on earth to gain a true perspective, through the eyes of faith, on the earthly conflict (and apparent defeat) that it is facing. John sees the armies of heaven (19:14) following the victorious Christ—another clue that the scene in 19:11–16 is a heavenly one. Since the parousia is not implied until 20:11, 20:1–6 describes realities, including the millennial period, that take place prior to Christ's physical return to earth.

On the basis of texts such as Matthew 12:29, John 12:31, and Colossians 2:15, it is argued that the "binding" of Satan occurred during the earthly ministry of Jesus, and particularly at the crucifixion. It is suggested that Satan has been bound in the sense that he is no longer able to prevent the spread of the gospel in the world (Hendriksen). The phrase *thousand years* is symbolic of the entire church age which extends from the resurrection and ascension of Christ until the final parousia. The number one thousand, being the cube of ten ($10 \times 10 \times 10$), is symbolic of completeness and perfection. This understanding of the phrase *thousand years,* it is argued, seems consistent with the usage of numbers elsewhere in the Apocalypse (e.g., "seven spirits," 1:4; "144,000," 7:4), usage that is evidently representative and symbolic in character.

The "thrones" (20:4) are taken to be located in heaven. Other references to thrones in Revelation refer to a heavenly setting (e.g., 4:2; 5:6–7, 13; 7:15; 11:16; 19:4–5). These texts in most instances refer to the throne of God, but 11:16 specifically relates to the twenty-four elders who sit

on heavenly thrones, suggestive of the church's participation in the reign of Christ (11:15; cf. 3:21; Eph. 2:6).

The "souls" (20:4) seen by John, in contrast to the "*flesh
of all men*" referred to in 19:18, is taken to indicate a
spiritual form of existence. The "coming to life" (20:4) of
those who share in the "first resurrection" refers either to
the soul's presence with Christ in the intermediate state
(Kline, Hughes), or to the believer's rising to new spiritual
life at conversion (Shepherd).

It is pointed out that Scripture elsewhere can use the
imagery of resurrection to describe new spiritual life.
Ezekiel 37:1–14 describes Israel's restoration from cap-
tivity in Babylon as a resurrection: "Behold, I will open
your graves, and raise you from your graves, O my people;
and I will bring you home into the land of Israel" (Ezek.
37:12). In the parable of the lost son the father speaks of
the prodigal's repentance as a type of resurrection: "this
your brother was dead, and is alive; he was lost, and is
found" (Luke 15:32). In the Gospel of John, Jesus speaks of
conversion in the language of resurrection: "Truly, truly, I
say to you, the hour is coming, *and now is,* when the dead
will hear the voice of the Son of God, and those who hear
will live" (5:25, italics added).

This nonliteral understanding of the "first resurrection," it is argued, is in keeping with other scriptural passages such as John 5:28–29 which clearly seem to indicate
a simultaneous resurrection of the righteous and the
wicked: "the *hour* is coming when *all* who are in the tombs
will hear his voice and come forth, those who have done
good, to the resurrection of life, and those who have done
evil, to the resurrection of judgment" (italics added). Such
an approach to Revelation 20:4–6 also has the merit of
showing the compatibility of the Apocalypse with the eschatological teachings of Jesus and Paul, who nowhere
explicitly speak of a thousand-year earthly reign and two
separate bodily resurrections.[8]

---

8. See especially the article by Page (n. 7) on the striking parallels between
Pauline eschatology and Rev. 20 when understood along amillennial lines.

Synthesis and Conclusions

Having reviewed some of the major features of the pre-millennial and amillennial approaches to the interpretation of Revelation 20:4–6, it now remains to draw these various strands together and to attempt to reach some conclusions.

At the outset it can be stated that the Book of Revelation as a whole presents the persecuted church with a theology of martyrdom, perhaps the most extensive such theology in the New Testament. In the opening salutation Jesus Christ is presented as "the faithful witness, the firstborn of the dead, and the ruler of kings on earth" (1:5). Already in the opening lines of the Apocalypse key themes of the book are foreshadowed: those who, like Christ himself, are faithful witnesses, even though they are martyred for their faith, will rise again from death, and will reign with him over the kings of the earth. The promise to the believers at Laodicea is likewise programmatic: "He who conquers, I will grant him to sit with me on my throne, as I myself conquered and sat down with my Father on his throne" (3:21). And how is it that the believer "conquers"? John's answer is stated in 12:11: "And they have conquered [Satan] by the blood of the Lamb and by the word of their testimony, for they loved not their lives even unto death." The martyrs are given the assurance that through their death they will participate in the victory of the risen Christ, who himself was the Lamb who was slain (5:6), and yet through his death conquered (5:5) and now has received all honor and glory and might for ever and ever (5:13).

Most New Testament scholars believe that the Revelation was written to give encouragement to Christians facing persecution and martyrdom during the reign of the emperor Domitian, during the closing years of the first century. In John's unique perspective, time and eternity, heaven and earth, are brought together through the believer's faith in and union with the risen Christ.[9] John's vision of the "heavens opened" allows the suffering church on earth to understand its experience from God's heavenly perspective,[10] and in the light of Christ's own death and resurrection: martyrdom through faithful witness is the sign not of the persecutor's triumph, but rather of his defeat.

John has taken apocalyptic imagery from the Book of Daniel and other Old Testament writings and reshaped these motifs in light of the central vision of the crucified, risen, and reigning Christ. As Brevard S. Childs has noted, this Old Testament imagery now serves the function of "identifying the defeated enemies of God and of the church who act from an earthbound perspective as if they were still in control."[11] Indeed the paradoxical yet fundamentally encouraging message of the book is this: death through martyrdom is truly conquest over the evil one; apparent earthly defeat for the church is the road to victory; the apparently irresistible earthly powers have already been defeated by the blood of the heavenly Lamb. "Through martyrdom unto victory" could well serve as the motto of the book.

The comments to follow will present an interpretation of Revelation 20:4–6 that reflects the general postmillennial perspective, relying for the most part on evidence which is internal to the book itself.

Concerning the chronological relationship of chapters

---

9. On this point see especially the essay by Paul S. Minear, "The Cosmology of the Apocalypse," in *Current Issues in New Testament Interpretation: Essays in Honor of Otto A. Piper,* ed. William Klassen and Graydon F. Snyder (New York: Harper and Brothers, 1962), pp. 23–37.

10. One might recall in this connection the prologue to the Book of Job, which allows the reader to see from an "upper-story," heavenly perspective the significance of the protagonist's earthly suffering.

11. Brevard S. Childs, *The New Testament as Canon: An Introduction* (Philadelphia: Fortress, 1984), p. 515.

19 and 20, 19:11–21 is understood to refer to the heavenly Christ's progressive victory over the forces of history prior to the parousia (cf. 1 Cor. 15:24b–25). The phrase *I saw heaven opened* (v. 11; cf. Acts 7:56) is taken as a clue that the vision describes the presence of the risen Christ in heaven and his spiritual warfare against his foes from that location. The reference to the great white throne (20:11) of judgment implies the return of Christ to judge the world (cf. Matt. 25:31). The binding of Satan and the millennial reign described in 20:1–6 consequently take place prior to the return of Christ to earth. Chapter 21, with the references to a new heaven and a new earth (v. 1) and the absence of death and pain (v. 4), describes the conditions of the eternal state subsequent to the general resurrection and last judgment.

The "binding" of Satan mentioned in 20:2 is understood to refer to a future event. Although it is true, as amillennialists point out, that Satan was bound in some sense during the earthly ministry of Christ (Matt. 12:29; John 12:31; Col. 2:15), John here apparently has in mind something more specific: a complete cessation of Satan's earthly influence. At the time when John was writing, Satan was quite active, and was about to throw some of the believers in Smyrna into prison—through the human instrumentality of persecuting Jews (2:9–10). The language of "shutting" and "sealing" in 20:3 implies a complete quarantining of the great enemy of God's people. Specifically, the "binding" means that Satan will "deceive the nations no more" (20:3) and will be unable to organize the nations in opposition to the church (20:8). Even after the crucifixion and resurrection, Satan was still able to stir up persecution against the Christian church (cf. 1 Peter 5:8, "Your adversary the devil prowls around like a roaring lion, seeking some one to devour," and 1 John 5:19, "the whole world is in the power of the evil one"). Satan's power was in principle broken at the cross (Col. 2:15), but he still engages in dangerous rearguard action prior to his destruction.

This understanding of the binding in 20:2 is consistent with John's usage of the same term *(deo)* in 9:14, where the sixth angel is told to "release the four angels who are bound at the great river Euphrates." After being released, the four avenging angels go forth to kill a third of mankind (9:15). The usage of the terms for "binding" and "releasing" in this context makes it clear that being "bound" means an inability to exert harmful (or deadly) influence on mankind. It is evident, then, on the basis of John's own usage of *deo,* that "inability to prevent the spread of the gospel" (Hendriksen) is simply too weak a meaning for the binding in Revelation 20:2. This binding refers to a particular spiritual event in the heavenly realm, subsequent to the earthly ministry of Jesus, and yet future from the perspective of the church, which will place a complete quarantine on Satan's activities. God will accomplish this binding through the instrumentality of an angel (Michael?; 20:1; cf. 12:7), and the millennium, an unprecedented period of peace and influence for the church, will then ensue.

The "thousand years" (20:4–6) could possibly be a literal thousand-year period, but in light of the usage of numbers in Revelation, more likely is a long period of spiritual prosperity for the church. John speaks of 144,000 sealed out of every tribe of the sons of Israel (7:4). In 11:13, 7,000 are killed in an earthquake. In 14:3, 144,000 are redeemed from the earth. In 21:16 the heavenly city measures twelve thousand stadia (about fifteen hundred miles) on each side. The fact that such numbers are multiples of seven, ten, and twelve strongly suggests that they are intended to symbolize the spiritual qualities of completeness, fullness, and perfection.

John gives no unambiguous indication of where the "thrones" (20:4) are located. On the one hand, the twenty-four elders, representative of the church, sit on heavenly thrones (11:16); and yet on the other hand in 5:10 it is said that the martyrs will reign on earth. But even in 5:10 there is no explicit reference to thrones, as in 20:4. It is also the case that there is no explicit reference anywhere in 20:1–6 to a physical presence of Christ on earth. Premillennial interpreters assume that the phrase *they . . . reigned with Christ a thousand years* (20:4b) presupposes Christ's second advent and presence on earth, but this is not actually stated in 20:1–6.

The crucial exegetical issue in this passage, as Ladd and others have pointed out, is the meaning of the terms *they came to life (ezēsan)* and *first resurrection* in verses 4–6. On this point the premillennial school appears to have the better argument, at least at the level of the literal force of the language. John uses this exact term *(ezēsan)* in 2:8, where it refers to the bodily resurrection of Jesus. Ladd is also correct in arguing that nothing in the context of 20:4–6 requires that *ezēsan* have a different meaning in verse 4 than it does in verse 5. Furthermore, with respect to the "first resurrection" *(hē anastasis hē prōtē),* it is the case that *anastasis* (resurrection, rising) is used forty-two times in the New Testament, and only in one case is it clearly metaphorical. In Luke 2:34 Simeon says to Mary, "This child is set for the fall and rising of many in Israel"— but here the context clearly points to a metaphorical sense. Thus it would seem that the "first resurrection" must be a literal, bodily resurrection at the beginning of the millennial period.

On the other hand, it can be argued that this conclusion is based on two assumptions, both of which can be questioned: first, that physical imagery requires an exclusively physical, literal meaning; and second, that bodily resurrection is exclusively future for the believer, even when God's perspective is taken into account.

On the first point, it is worthwhile to note that in 20:1–2 the terms *key, chain,* and *dragon* are certainly physical images, but are clearly physical images of spiritual real-

ities. It has already been noted that in Ezekiel 37:12 the
language of bodily resurrection ("I will . . . raise you from
your graves") is used to state a spiritual truth, that is, the
promise of Israel's restoration from exile in Babylon. Furthermore, the striking parallel between the events described in Ezekiel 37–38 and Revelation 20:4–10 makes it
almost certain that John saw in Ezekiel's prophecy the
background of his own vision.[12] In a metaphorical yet spiritually real sense, Israel's restoration from exile was a
"resurrection" (Ezek. 37:1–14). Likewise, the restoration
and vindication in history of the cause for which the martyrs died is the "first resurrection." The "second resurrection" (implied, but not explicitly mentioned by John in
20:4–6) is the bodily resurrection at the end of the age.

Although it is true that nothing in the immediate context of 20:4–6 implies different meanings for *ezēsan* in
verses 4 and 5, the clear evidence of Ezekiel 37–38 as Old
Testament background for 20:4–10 does give support for a
nonliteral understanding of the "first resurrection."

On the second point, although it is true that "resurrection" in Jewish thought is essentially bodily resurrection,
it should also be noted that events (such as resurrection)
which are yet future from the human perspective can be
seen as already present and realized to God. Notable here
is the statement of Jesus in Matthew 22:31–32, in the
context of a dispute with the Sadducees on the resurrection: "And as for the resurrection of the dead, have you not
read what was said to you by God, 'I am the God of Abraham, and the God of Isaac, and the God of Jacob'? He is not

---

12. It is quite significant that the sequence of events described in Ezek.
37–38 (restoration as "resurrection," 37:1–14; a period of peace and unity
under the new Davidic king, 37:15–28; the hordes of Gog assembled and
defeated, 38) is closely paralleled in Rev. 20:4–10 ("first resurrection"; a period
of peace and victory; the final assault of Gog and Magog, and their defeat by
God). It is difficult to imagine that John did not have Ezek. 37–38 in mind as
the background to Rev. 20:4–10, and this gives further weight to the metaphorical understanding of the "first resurrection" (20:5).

God of the dead, but of the living." Christ proves the resurrection from Exodus 3:6, citing from texts accepted by the Sadducees as authoritative. From a human perspective, Abraham, Isaac, and Jacob are dead in the grave, and their resurrection is still future. But from God's perspective, they live (v. 32b) and have already been resurrected. In God's sight the patriarchs have already been resurrected—otherwise Christ's citation of Exodus 3:6 and the remark about God as the God of the living in the context of a dispute about the resurrection of the dead would have been pointless. This type of argumentation on our Lord's part, which strikes the modern reader of the Bible as strange and artificial, is in fact an example of the paradox of the "already" and the "not yet" in the New Testament. As Paul states elsewhere, we have already been resurrected with Christ in a spiritual sense (Eph. 2:6; Col. 2:12; 3:1), even though we have not yet experienced the final bodily resurrection at the end of the age.

Consequently, the "first resurrection" in 20:5–6 can be seen paradoxically as both physical and spiritual, as both future and present. Physical imagery is used to express a spiritual truth; in the sight of God, the bodily resurrection of the martyrs is a present reality (like Abraham's, Matt. 22:32), while to the church below, it is still a future hope.

This same spiritual paradox of the "already" and the "not yet" is also seen in John's theology of martyrdom. In one sense the saints' conquering of the evil one points to a future hope: "He who conquers and who keeps my works until the end, I will give him power over the nations" (2:26). At the same time, and perhaps in a more profound sense, the martyrs have already conquered Satan through their very martyrdom: "And they *have conquered* him by the blood of the Lamb and by the word of their testimony, for they loved not their lives even unto death" (12:11, italics added).

These conclusions are in keeping with those of Mounce, one of the most able of recent premillennial commentators on the Apocalypse. According to Mounce, the essential meaning of 20:4–6 is that "the martyr's steadfastness will win for him the highest life in union with God and Christ." Alluding to a distinction between the outward form of prophetic language and its spiritual import, Mounce recognizes that John used the imagery of a literal millennium, but concludes that "its essential meaning may be realized in something other than a temporal fulfillment."[13] This general approach also has the advantage of showing consistency between the eschatological teaching of Revelation and that of Jesus, Paul, John, and the other New Testament writers.

The "first resurrection," then, refers to the future restoration and vindication of the cause for which the martyrs died. In one sense they already reign with Christ (Eph. 2:6), but in a more specific sense, during the future millennial period of blessing for the church, they will share, from their heavenly thrones, the honor of reigning with Christ. "Blessed and holy is he who shares in the first resurrection!" (20:6).

At the end of the millennial period Satan will be loosed from prison and will deceive the nations, gathering them for battle (20:7–8). Christ will destroy Satan at his coming (20:9b; cf. 2 Thess. 2:8) and cast him into the lake of fire (20:10). The apostasy described by John in 20:7–8 is elsewhere spoken of in Scripture in 2 Thessalonians 2:1–7 and Luke 17:26–30, passages which describe conditions on earth immediately prior to the parousia. At the return of Christ the dead are raised and the last judgment occurs (20:11–15), and then God ushers in the eternal state (21–22).

---

13. Mounce, *The Book of Revelation*, p. 359. Note, for example, the statement in Mal. 4:5, "Behold, I will send you Elijah the prophet before the great and terrible day of the Lord comes." Malachi may have thought of a literal visitation of Elijah, but in Matt. 11:13–14 Christ indicates that the prophecy was fulfilled in a spiritual sense in the ministry of John the Baptist ("if you are willing to accept it, he is Elijah who is to come").

Finally, it should be stated that even if the reader of Revelation 20:4–6 should still favor a premillennial interpretation, there is no reason to conclude that the Apocalypse is basically pessimistic concerning the church's prospects in history, or that Revelation 20 is totally incompatible with the hopeful outlook represented by the postmillennial view. It has been argued here that Christology is the key to biblical eschatology and the Christian hope for the future, and John sees the risen Christ as the victorious "King of kings and Lord of lords" (19:16). The Book of Revelation is clear, to be sure, that the church's experience in history includes tribulation, persecution, and even martyrdom. But at the same time, the seer's vision which begins with seven struggling congregations in Asia Minor (2–3) ends with the magnificent vision of an incredibly expansive New Jerusalem that boggles the imagination (21:9–22:5). Those who come through great tribulation are a great multitude of the redeemed that no man can number (7:9). All nations will come to worship before God Almighty and the Lamb (15:4). There are shadows in abundance in the Apocalypse, but in the last analysis, these dark elements of the church's experience in history are far outweighed by the light of the risen Christ's glorious triumph. The overall message of Revelation is indeed "through tribulation unto victory."

6

Contrary Texts
in the New Testament

According to Millard J. Erickson, one of the difficulties with the postmillennial position is that it tends to neglect biblical passages that "portray spiritual and moral conditions as worsening in the end times."[1] There are also many New Testament texts that appear to portray the return of Christ as imminent. Could the postmillennial outlook, which suggests a long period of time prior to the second advent, possibly be consistent with such texts? And finally, what of texts which appear to teach that the number of the faithful will be small when Christ returns (e.g., Luke 18:8, "When the Son of man comes, will he find faith on earth?")?

Any viable eschatological framework must take into account all the relevant biblical data. This chapter will attempt to show how the types of texts mentioned are understood within a postmillennial framework.

---

1. Millard J. Erickson, *Contemporary Options in Eschatology: A Study of the Millennium* (Grand Rapids: Baker, 1977), p. 72.

"Behold, the Judge Is Standing at the Doors"

The New Testament contains many passages which express a sense of the nearness of the return of Christ. This sense of the imminency of the parousia is the basis for ethical exhortations for the believer to maintain an attitude of watchfulness and spiritual alertness. "Watch therefore, for you do not know on what day your Lord is coming. . . . Therefore you also must be ready; for the Son of man is coming at an hour you do not expect" (Matt. 24:42, 44).

Such an awareness of the nearness of the end is also pervasive in the Epistles. Paul writes to the Christians in Rome that "salvation is nearer to us now than when we first believed; the night is far gone, the day is at hand" (Rom. 13:11–12). Marriage may be inexpedient for some in Corinth, since "the appointed time has grown very short" (1 Cor. 7:29). In his first letter to the Thessalonian church, the apostle appears to include himself among those who will still be alive at the time of the advent: "we who are alive, who are left until the coming of the Lord, shall not precede [in the rapture] those who have fallen asleep" (1 Thess. 4:15).[2]

This sense of imminency can also be seen in the general Epistles. James warns the community not to grumble against one another, in order to avoid Christ's judgment, inasmuch as "the Judge is standing at the doors" (James 5:9). Peter exhorts the Christians in Asia Minor to keep sane and sober for prayer since "the end of all things is at hand" (1 Peter 4:7). The Johannine community is warned

---

2. On the question of development over time in Paul's eschatology, see Richard N. Longenecker, "The Nature of Paul's Early Eschatology," *New Testament Studies* 31 (1985): 85–95. Longenecker does see some development in Paul's eschatology, but argues that the apostle's primary commitment "was not first of all to a program or some timetable of events but to a person: Jesus the Messiah" (p. 93). In other words, the primary emphasis of Pauline eschatology is christological, not calendrical.

about the coming of false teachers, whose very presence is evidence that it is the "last hour" (1 John 2:18).

The closing lines of the Apocalypse contain the promise of the risen Christ, "Surely I am coming soon" (Rev. 22:20).

There are various ways in which the interpreter of Scripture can respond to this sense of imminency expressed in texts that are now almost two thousand years old. Some scholars have concluded that Jesus and/or his followers were simply mistaken on the question of the time of the second advent—a mistake that is understandable given the limitations of human nature and historical circumstances.[3] Others have suggested that the belief in an imminent parousia may have been produced by the (mistaken) activity of itinerant prophets in the early church.[4] It has also been argued that the parousia already took place in A.D. 70 when, through the instrumentality of the Roman armies, Christ came spiritually in judgment upon Jerusalem. The New Testament texts have reference to this event, and not to some yet future advent.[5]

These approaches are not consistent with the evangelical tradition of interpretation as generally understood, and do not appear to be required by the texts themselves. A more adequate approach to the question of the imminency of the parousia and its bearing on the postmillennial understanding would include a variety of different considerations, the more important of which include the following:

First, God's perspective on time is not the same as our own, as 2 Peter 3:8 makes clear: "with the Lord one day is as a thousand years, and a thousand years as one day." The allusion here is to Psalm 90:4, a psalm which contrasts

---

3. See, for example, H. P. Owen, "The Parousia of Christ in the Synoptic Gospels," *Scottish Journal of Theology* 12 (1959): 171–92.

4. J. G. Davies, "The Genesis of Belief in an Imminent Parousia," *Journal of Theological Studies* n.s. 14 (1963): 104–7.

5. J. Stuart Russell, *The Parousia: A Study of the New Testament Doctrine of Our Lord's Second Coming* (reprint ed.; Grand Rapids: Baker, 1983).

God's eternity and man's transience. The apparent delay in Christ's parousia is actually an expression of God's mercy, for he wished that even the scoffers (v. 3) would reach repentance.[6] From God's point of view, the span between the first century and our own is only several "days," and God in his mercy may well ordain many more such "days" in the future to complete his purpose of bringing the gospel of repentance to all.

Second, there is the phenomenon in Scripture that has been termed "telescoping" or "compression" of immediate historical judgments and the ultimate judgment which they prefigure. The prophet Joel, on the occasion of a locust plague devasting Judah (Joel 1:4), states that "the day of the LORD is coming, it is near" (2:1). Some twenty-five hundred years later, the ultimate judgment is yet to come. Evidently the prophet saw in the locust plague a prefiguring of the final judgment, and the two events are superimposed in his outlook.[7] The reality and certainty of impending divine judgment are expressed in the existential sense of "nearness." A similar phenomenon may be observed in Isaiah 61:2, where the prophet compresses the first and second advent. The servant of the Lord comes to "proclaim the year of the LORD's favor, and the day of ven-

---

6. Charles H. Talbert, "II Peter and the Delay of the Parousia," *Vigilae Christianae* 20 (1966): 137–45, has perceptively pointed out that nowhere does the author say that the whole church was disturbed by a "delayed Parousia," as most scholars tend to assume. Rather, the only ones who appear to consider the delay of the parousia a problem are the heretics, the outsiders (3:3–4). These Gnostics advocated a realized-spiritualized eschatology, and hence were disturbed by the hope of a yet future parousia, a parousia bringing judgment on the lifestyles displayed by the scoffers. Talbert concludes that 2 Peter "cannot be used as evidence for the thesis that the delay of the Parousia caused a crisis of major proportions in the life and thought of early Christianity" (p. 145). See also Richard J. Bauckham, "The Delay of the Parousia," *Tyndale Bulletin* 31 (1980): 3–36.

7. K. F. Keil, *Biblical Commentary on the Old Testament* (25 vols.), *The Twelve Minor Prophets*, trans. James Martin, 2 vols. (Grand Rapids: Eerdmans, 1949), vol. 1, p. 190: "Joel now proclaims the coming of that day in its full completion, on the basis of the judgment already experienced." The coming of the day of Jehovah is represented as "indisputably certain" (p. 189).

geance of our God." Significantly, in Luke 4:18–19, in Luke's account of Jesus' appearance at the synagogue in Nazareth, the Lord reads from the Isaiah scroll, but stops at 61:2a ("the acceptable year of the Lord"), and omits 61:2b ("the day of vengeance of our God"). Christ distinguished his first advent in mercy from the second in judgment, whereas Isaiah had superimposed the two. It may be that New Testament texts expressing the sense of the imminency of the parousia could likewise "foreshorten" the time between the ascension of Christ and the end of all things.

Third, it should be observed that the New Testament contains not only texts expressing a sense of imminency, but also those which speak of possible delay. The parable of the faithful and unfaithful servants (Matt. 24:45–51; Luke 12:42–46) has the wicked servant saying to himself, "My master is delayed" (Matt. 24:48). In the parable of the ten virgins, the maidens all slumbered and slept as the bridegroom was delayed (Matt. 25:5). In the parable of the talents (Matt. 25:14–30) it is stated that "after a long time" (v. 19) the master returned from his journey and settled accounts with the servants to whom he had entrusted his property. Such texts reminded the early church that the sense of the nearness of the end had to be held in tension with the possibility of the master's delay.

Significantly, the exhortations to watchfulness in the New Testament are predicated not so much on the known chronological nearness of the parousia as on its unexpectedness—for example, Matthew 24:44, "Therefore you also must be ready; for the Son of man is coming at an hour *you do not expect*" (italics added). The day of the Lord will come like "a thief in the night" (1 Thess. 5:2)—that is, unexpectedly. It is this unexpectedness and uncertainty of the time of the end, rather than any human ability to calculate its time on the calendar, which is the foundation for the admonitions to remain alert and spiritually awake.

Fourth, the New Testament does speak of events which

are to precede the end and which imply a significant interval between the ascension of Christ and his final coming in glory. The gospel is to be preached throughout the whole world as a testimony to the nations before the end comes (Matt. 24:14; cf. Luke 24:47).[8] While it can be argued that in a sense this has already been accomplished, the gospel having been preached throughout the entire known world (the Roman Empire) in Paul's own day (Col. 1:6), the gospel texts would appear to imply a more truly universal sense of the "whole world." Surely the commission to make disciples of "all nations" (Matt. 28:19) was intended by Christ to extend beyond the boundaries of the Roman Empire, especially in light of the global authority of Christ ("all authority in heaven and on earth," v. 18) that is the foundation of the commission. The mandate is to extend Christ's kingdom throughout the earth, for his authority extends over all without exception. The author of the Apocalypse states that the blood of the Lamb has ransomed men for God from every tongue and tribe and people and nation (Rev. 5:9). A countless multitude from every nation, from all tribes and peoples and tongues (Rev. 7:9), is seen standing before the heavenly throne, acclaiming God and the Lamb for the salvation that has been wrought. The global reach of such language is difficult to deny and implies a considerable task that is yet to be completed by the church in its missionary tasks.

Fifth, it should be noted that Christ can come at any time in providential judgment upon a nation, church, or individual. In the Old Testament God comes spiritually yet truly in judgment on rebellious nations. In an oracle concerning Egypt, Isaiah says, "Behold, the LORD is riding on a swift cloud and comes to Egypt" (Isa. 19:1). God was

---

8. Richard H. Hiers, "The Delay of the Parousia in Luke-Acts," *New Testament Studies* 20 (1974): 154: "Luke . . . makes it clear that Jesus did not look for the Parousia until the gentile mission had been completed: 24:46; Acts 1:6–8."

not physically present, but Nebuchadnezzar did invade Egypt about 568 B.C., and as such was the human instrument of the divine judgment. Through the instrumentality of the Roman armies of Titus, God came in judgment upon rebellious Jerusalem in A.D. 70 and the resulting devastation fulfilled the prophecy of Christ recorded in Matthew 24:1–2. The risen Christ warns the church at Ephesus that "I will come to you and remove your lampstand from its place, unless you repent" (Rev. 2:5). Those at Pergamum receive a similar warning: "Repent then. If not, I will come to you soon and war against them with the sword of my mouth" (Rev. 2:16). The reference to the "sword of my mouth" is figurative language (cf. 1:16), but the spiritual coming in judgment is very real in its effects. Certain individuals in Corinth who were abusing the Lord's Supper experienced the judgment of Christ, to the point of illness and even death (1 Cor. 11:29–32). The risen Christ who is now at the right hand of the Father and who will return at the end of history as the Judge of the world is also the one whose presence is felt in judgment by nations, churches, and individuals within history. The reality of Christ's spiritual visitations in judgment in history provides a sober warning to the church to maintain its watchfulness and spiritual vigilance.

Sixth, and most importantly, the sense of the imminency of the parousia in the New Testament is to be understood in terms of the reality of Christ's finished victory at the cross and the powerful presence of the Holy Spirit in the church. The early church had a vivid sense of the nearness of the end because, in a very real sense, the final events of the end had already come in Jesus. In the preaching of Jesus the kingdom of God had drawn near (Mark 1:15). Satan's power had been stripped away at the cross (Col. 2:15), and the death of Christ had abolished death (2 Tim. 1:10). The final events of the end are, as A. L. Moore has pointed out, "already accomplished in

Christ."[9] Furthermore, the Holy Spirit in the church not only communicates to the believer the reality of Christ's past work, but the presence of the Spirit is a sign of the end as well, and "an assurance that the present is already . . . an anticipation of the Last Age."[10] The "first fruits" of the Spirit (Rom. 8:23) experienced by the believer now make real the complete redemption of the age to come. The New Testament writers had a vivid sense of imminency, but nowhere set dates for the parousia. They realized, as Moore has noted, that "the time for repentance and faith could not be limited by men and that the provision of God's mercy could not be measured or forecast."[11] The sense of the imminency of the parousia in the New Testament, then, is fundamentally christological and existential rather than chronological and calendrical in nature. The nearness of Christ cannot be adequately understood in terms of simple linear time. Our normal temporal categories have been collapsed by the cross, resurrection, and sending of the Holy Spirit. The spiritual realities help us to understand the paradoxical combination of New Testament expressions of the nearness of the end and, at the same time, warnings of delay—a delay that is itself an expression of God's sovereign grace and mercy, and the time of the church's mission.

"In the Last Days, There Will Come Times of Stress"

Is world history "running downhill"? Does the Bible teach that world conditions will steadily deteriorate with

---

9. A. L. Moore, *The Parousia in the New Testament* (Leiden: E. J. Brill, 1966), p. 168. Moore's excellent treatment points out the weakness of much recent New Testament scholarship, which frequently tends to assume that Jesus and the early church were simply mistaken in their eschatological expectations.

10. Ibid., p. 169.

11. Ibid., pp. 206–7.

the passage of time, and that this decline will be climaxed with an unparalleled time of worldwide, violent persecution of Christians ("the great tribulation") immediately prior to the return of Christ? Many scriptural passages have been interpreted in such a sense.

Writing to the Christians in Galatia, the apostle Paul speaks of the "present evil age" (Gal. 1:4). John declares that "the whole world is in the power of the evil one" (1 John 5:19). Jesus warns the disciples that in the world they will have tribulation (John 16:33). In the last days there will indeed come times of stress (2 Tim. 3:1). In the Olivet discourse the Lord speaks of a time of "great tribulation, such as has not been from the beginning of the world until now, no, and never will be" (Matt. 24:21). In the face of such biblical statements, is it possible to maintain an optimistic hope for the future course of human history?

The statements of Galatians 1:4 and 1 John 5:19 need to be seen as realistic descriptions of Satan's continuing rearguard actions in the world. It is true that Satan still prowls about like a roaring lion, seeking someone to devour (1 Peter 5:8). But more fundamentally, Satan's power is a broken power, and his authority a pseudo-authority. Satan has been decisively defeated at the cross of Christ (Col. 2:15). John also confidently writes that "he who is in you is greater than he who is in the world" (1 John 4:4). Whoever is born of God overcomes the world, and "this is the victory that overcomes the world, our faith" (1 John 5:4). Raymond E. Brown observes that "the author means that Christian conquest is inevitable, flowing from the fact that the world has already been conquered by Jesus."[12]

Paul may speak of the "present evil age," but this does not produce passivity and resignation in his own ministry

---

12. Raymond E. Brown, *The Epistles of John* (Garden City, N.Y.: Doubleday, 1982), p. 572. In a similar vein, I. Howard Marshall, *The Epistles of John* (Grand Rapids: Eerdmans, 1978), p. 229, comments: "Such faith is far from being wish-fulfillment . . . it rests foursquare on the fact that Jesus Christ has defeated death, and anybody who can defeat death can defeat anything."

or in his hope for the church. He knows that the power of
Christ is far greater than that of the evil one. He knows
that the spiritual weapons of his apostolic ministry have
"divine power to destroy strongholds" and can take every
thought captive to Christ (2 Cor. 10:4, 5). Satan has been
defeated, and Paul writes to the Christians in Rome that
"the God of peace will soon crush Satan under your feet"
(Rom. 16:20). This is hardly the voice of historical pessimism!

It is indeed true that in the world Christians experience
tribulation (John 16:33; Rom. 8:35), as the history of the
church has attested. But tribulation is not to be identified
with defeat of Christ's cause on earth. Tribulation there
may be, but Christ has overcome the world (John 16:33b).
Those who are called to martyrdom in fact conquer the evil
one by the blood of the Lamb and by the word of their
testimony (Rev. 12:11).

Will tribulation, especially in the sense of bloody persecution, intensify as the end draws near? Is this the sense
of 2 Timothy 3:1, "in the last days there will come times of
stress"? With respect to this text, several observations are
in order. First, Paul states that the ungodly behavior that
is to be prominent in the end time is already apparent;
Timothy is warned to "avoid" the ungodly (2 Tim. 3:5). The
church is already living in the end time, which extends
from the resurrection of Christ to the parousia (cf. Heb.
1:2, "in these last days"), and such times of "stress" are
manifested in various degrees of intensity throughout the
church age.

Second, it is significant that there is nowhere in 2 Timothy 3:1–8 any explicit mention of violent persecution of
Christians. Burton Scott Easton notes that "overt crimes
are omitted from the list of vices, and nothing is said about
physical 'woes' such as eclipses, earthquakes, pestilence,"
and so forth.[13] Rather, the characteristic features of the

---

13. Burton Scott Easton, *The Pastoral Epistles* (London: SCM, 1948), p. 63.

time appear to be hedonism, materialism, egotism, and hypocrisy in religion: "lovers of self, lovers of money . . . lovers of pleasure rather than lovers of God, holding the form of religion but denying the power of it" (vv. 2, 4–5). This picture is quite consistent with Christ's description of worldly conditions immediately prior to the end (Luke 17:26–30). During the days of Noah and of Lot, the picture was one of apparent normalcy: eating, drinking, marrying, giving in marriage, buying, selling, planting, building (vv. 27–28)—but then sudden judgment came. This picture of a careless and complacent generation of unbelievers immediately prior to the parousia is given as well by Paul in 1 Thessalonians 5:3: "When people say, 'There is *peace and security,*' then sudden destruction will come upon them . . . and there will be no escape" (italics added). Leon Morris notes that the present tense of *legōsin* in verse 3 indicates that "they will still be saying these words at the very moment when the 'sudden destruction' comes."[14]

These three texts (2 Tim. 3:1–5; Luke 17:26–30; and 1 Thess. 5:3) teach, then, that immediately prior to the parousia the church is not to look so much for "war and rumors of wars," great violent persecution, and social turmoil, but rather for the more insidious spiritual threat of complacency, worldliness, materialism, and hedonism.[15] A postmillennial framework can incorporate these texts, inasmuch as within this framework there is a final apostasy and deceiving of the nations (Rev. 20:7–8; 2 Thess. 2:9–11) immediately prior to the second advent and after

---

Martin Dibelius and Hans Conzelmann, *The Pastoral Epistles: A Commentary on the Pastoral Epistles,* ed. Helmut Koester, trans. Philip Buttolph and Adela Yarbro (Philadelphia: Fortress, 1972), p. 116, note that the list of vices "is in many ways reminiscent of Rom. 1:30f."

14. Leon Morris, *The First and Second Epistles to the Thessalonians* (Grand Rapids: Eerdmans, 1959), p. 153.

15. Likewise, in 2 Thess. 1:1–11, the great threat to the church is not overt persecution, but wicked deception (v. 10) inspired by Satan himself: the threat of false religion.

the period of millennial blessing on the church (Rev.
20:4–6). Indeed, the very conditions of temporal prosperity
which are a secondary effect of the millennial blessings
make the worldliness and carelessness described in
2 Timothy 3:1–5, Luke 17:26–30, and 1 Thessalonians 5:3
understandable but not excusable. Vast numbers of nominal believers and professing unbelievers grow proud and
careless because of their worldly prosperity, and even the
church is sorely tested by conditions of affluence in the
millennial period. Church history and the experience of
Christians in Europe and North America indeed under-
score the truth that affluence can be a greater threat to the
vitality of faith than bloody persecution and open afflic- .
tion.

What about the "great tribulation" spoken of in the
Olivet discourse (Matt. 24:21; Mark 13:19; Luke 21:23)?
The position taken here is that Jesus in this section of the
discourse (Matt. 24:15–26) is referring specifically to
the devastation of Jerusalem in A.D. 70 by the armies of
the Roman general Titus.[16] In verses 1–2 of this chapter
Jesus specifically refers to the destruction of the temple.
The references to the holy place, Judea, and the sabbath
(vv. 15–16, 20) clearly identify the location of the tribulation as Judea (v. 21), and more specifically, Jerusalem. In
his parallel treatment of the Olivet discourse Luke makes
it especially clear that the tribulation spoken of refers to
God's judgment upon the unbelieving Jews: "For great distress shall be upon the earth [or, land; gēs] and wrath *upon
this people*" (21:23, italics added).

It might be thought that the specific language of Matthew 24:21, "great tribulation, *such as has not been from
the beginning of the world until now,* no, and *never will be*"

---

16. For this approach, see also J. Marcellus Kik, *An Eschatology of Victory*
(Nutley, N.J.: Presbyterian and Reformed, 1971); William Kimball, *The Great
Tribulation* (1983; Grand Rapids: Baker, 1984); William Barclay, "Matthew
24," *Expository Times* 70 (1959): 326–30; Ray Summers, "Matthew 24–25: An
Exposition," *Review and Expositor* 59 (1962): 501–11.

(italics added), could not possibly have found its fulfillment in A.D. 70. Specific knowledge concerning the siege of Jerusalem will modify this impression, however. "The final siege and fall of Jerusalem form one of the most terrible stories in all history," writes William Barclay.[17]

According to the Jewish historian Josephus, ninety-seven thousand Jews were taken captive by the Romans, and more than one million died during the siege by the sword or by slow starvation. Josephus describes the progress of the siege: "Then did the famine widen its progress, and devoured the people by whole houses and families; the upper rooms were full of women and children that were dying of famine; and the lanes of the city were full of the dead bodies of the aged; the children also and the young men wandered about the market-places like shadows, all swelled with the famine, and fell down dead wheresoever their misery seized them. As for burying them, those that were sick themselves were not able to do it; and those that were hearty and well were deterred from doing it by the great multitude of those dead bodies, and by the uncertainty there was how soon they should die themselves, for many died as they were burying others, and many went to their coffins before the fatal hour was come" (*Wars of the Jews*, 5.12.3). One woman was driven to such desperation during the siege that she killed, roasted, and ate her nursing child (6.3.4). Even the Romans were horrified when they entered the city and saw the conditions within: When the Romans "were come to the houses to plunder them, they found in them entire families of dead men, and the upper rooms full of dead corpses . . . they then stood in horror of this sight, and went out without touching anything" (6.8.5).

More Jews were killed in the Holocaust, but in the intensity and quality of the suffering, the siege of Jerusalem would appear to be unparalleled in recorded history. In-

17. Barclay, "Matthew 24," p. 327.

deed, God's wrath for all the righteous blood spilled on earth fell upon that generation (Matt. 23:36), as Christ had predicted.

It is true that Revelation 7:14 speaks of saints who come out of the great tribulation, but nowhere is it stated that this is a period specific to the end time. Tribulation is indeed an experience of saints throughout church history, as John himself attests: "I John, your brother . . . share with you in Jesus the tribulation and the kingdom" (Rev. 1:9). The "great tribulation" of Matthew 24:21, however, does not refer to a final worldwide, violent persecution immediately prior to the second advent, but rather to God's judgment in Jerusalem in A.D. 70.

"When the Son of Man Comes, Will He Find Faith on Earth?"

There are not only those texts that have been taken to imply a steady deterioration of conditions in the world with the passage of time; there are also those that appear to predict decline in the church as well. The text already cited (Luke 18:8) is one such passage, and there are others as well in the New Testament. In the Sermon on the Mount Christ tells the crowds that "the gate is narrow and the way is hard, that leads to life, and those who find it are few" (Matt. 7:14; cf. Luke 13:24, "Strive to enter by the narrow door"). Christ also stated that "many are called, but few are chosen" (Matt. 22:14). Can such texts be reconciled with the picture of vast numbers of people being converted to the Christian faith during a future period of great revival?

With respect to Luke 18:8, "when the Son of man comes, will he find faith on earth," it should be recalled that the postmillennial framework does recognize a period of apostasy and decline immediately prior to the parousia (Rev. 20:7–8; cf. 2 Thess. 2:1–11). It is to this period that Luke 18:8 is understood to refer. The preceding context (Luke

17:22–37) speaks of the complacency and carelessness that will be characteristic of society immediately prior to the end, and by implication Christ warns the disciples not to become infected by this worldly spirit.

In his commentary on this text Frederic Godet writes that we "must here remember the sad picture of the state of humanity at this epoch (17:26–30). Is it not to such a state of things that Jesus also makes allusion, Matt[hew] 25:5: 'And they *all* slumbered and slept?'"[18]

The period of apostasy immediately prior to the parousia, which will threaten to engulf even the faithful in spiritual complacency (Luke 18:8; Matt. 25:5), does not exclude a period of great revival before the final falling away. Indeed, the great revival of the church, and its secondary effects in particular—temporal peace and material prosperity (cf. Isa. 2:2–4; 65:20–25)—are the conditions that make the warnings about spiritual complacency so relevant. The saying in Luke 18:8 warns the believers to not let their faith waver, notwithstanding the apparent delay in the return of Christ,[19] and despite the spirit of worldliness around them (17:26–30).

The sayings concerning the narrow gate (Matt. 7:14), the narrow door (Luke 13:24), and the few who are chosen (Matt. 22:14) are best understood in the context of Jesus' own earthly ministry.[20] The "gate" or "door" that leads to eternal life is narrow in several respects. First, it is narrow theologically: Jesus, and Jesus alone, is the door to eternal life (John 10:7, "I am the door of the sheep"). The others who came before Christ are thieves and robbers (John

---

18. Frederic Godet, *A Commentary of the Gospel of St. Luke,* trans. M. D. Cusin, 5th ed., 2 vols. (reprint ed.; Edinburgh: T. and T. Clark, 1976), vol. 2, pp. 202–3.

19. Norval Geldenhuys, *Commentary on the Gospel of Luke* (Grand Rapids: Eerdmans, 1981), p. 447.

20. See Benjamin B. Warfield, "Are They Few that Be Saved?" in *Biblical and Theological Studies,* ed. Samuel G. Craig (Philadelphia: Presbyterian and Reformed, 1952), pp. 334–50.

10:8)—false prophets and messianic pretenders such as
Theudas and Judas the Galilean (Acts 5:36, 37)—who lead
the sheep astray. There is salvation in no one else but
Christ, and there is no other name under heaven given
among men by which we must be saved (Acts 4:12).

Second, the "gate" is narrow circumstantially, in that
few of the Jews responded savingly to the Lord's own
earthly ministry; indeed, he was "despised and rejected by
men" (Isa. 53:3). Many of the Jews were called to the messianic banquet (Matt. 22:14; also read vv. 1–13), but relatively few responded to the Lord himself.

These sayings (Matt. 7:14; Luke 13:24; Matt. 22:14),
then, must be seen against the backdrop of the limited
response of Israel to Christ's Palestinian ministry. They
are not intended to settle the issue of the ultimate outcome
and magnitude of Christ's redemptive work. The parables
of the mustard seed and the leaven (Matt. 13:31–33) indeed show that over the course of time Jesus expected
remarkable growth for the kingdom. The apostle Paul,
who is disappointed by the limited response of the Jews of
his own day, foresees a time when "all Israel will be saved"
(Rom. 11:26). John of the Apocalypse writes to churches
facing persecution and martyrdom, but is given the vision
of a countless multitude of the redeemed standing before
Christ's throne at the end of time (Rev. 7:9). Such texts help
us to see Matthew 7:14, Luke 13:24, and Matthew 22:14 in
the proper perspective, and prevent us from drawing pessimistic conclusions concerning the ultimate results of
Christ's redemptive work.

7

The Signs
of the Times

If present trends continue, the world in 2000 will be more crowded, more polluted, less stable ecologically, and more vulnerable to disruption than the world we live in now," concluded the authors of the *Global 2000 Report*. "Serious stresses involving population, resources, and environment are clearly visible ahead. Despite greater material output, the world's people will be poorer in many ways than they are today."[1]

The authors of *The Resourceful Earth: A Response to Global 2000*, are, however, more optimistic about the future: "We are confident that the nature of the physical world permits continued improvement in humankind's economic lot in the long run, indefinitely. . . . Sometimes temporary large-scale problems arise. But the nature of the world's physical conditions and the resilience in a

---

1. Gerald O. Barney, *The Global 2000 Report to the President,* 3 vols. (Washington, D.C.: U.S. Government Printing Office, 1980), vol. 1, p. 1.

well-functioning economic and social system enable us to overcome such problems, and the solutions usually leave us better off than if the problems had never arisen; that is the great lesson to be learned from human history."[2]

Which set of scientific forecasts is the layman to believe? How do our perceptions of world conditions influence our reading of the Bible and the formation of our beliefs about eschatology? Would deteriorating conditions in the world count as a decisive argument against postmillennialism, or improving conditions as an argument for it? These are some of the issues to be explored in the present chapter.

Hermeneutics or *Zeitgeist?*

"Time and again there seems to be a connection between eschatology and the Church's perception of itself in its historical situation," observed Stanley N. Gundry. "Eschatologies have been a reflection of the current mood or *Zeitgeist* or response to historical conditions."[3]

The more pessimistic premillennial outlook was popular in the first three centuries of the Christian church, when believers were periodically threatened with persecution, were social outcasts, and exercised little influence within the political system. Joseph Alsted, one of the earliest of the post-Reformation advocates of the premillennial position, had witnessed the devastation that the Thirty Years' War brought to Europe. The French Revolution and the Napoleonic Wars also contributed to the growing interest in premillennial interpretation. After the Civil War the problems of industrialization, urbanization, and immigration led many American Christians to adopt a less hopeful outlook, and the disillusionment caused by the First World War deepened the mood of his-

---

2. Julian L. Simon and Herman Kahn, eds., *The Resourceful Earth: A Response to Global 2000* (New York: Blackwell, 1984), p. 3.

3. Stanley N. Gundry, "Hermeneutics or *Zeitgeist* as the Determining Factor in the History of Eschatologies?" *Journal of the Evangelical Theological Society* 20:1 (1977): 50.

torical pessimism. The loss of denominational control by conservative Protestants during the Fundamentalist-Modernist controversies in the early part of the twentieth century may also have contributed to the attractiveness of such an eschatological outlook.

Postmillennialism, on the other hand, flourished when the churches were experiencing revival. This outlook reached its zenith in America prior to the Civil War, when Protestant churches were experiencing vigorous growth. The expanding American frontier, industrial growth, and new discoveries in transportation and communication all helped to produce an optimistic and expansive outlook in the churches. Postmillennialism remained the dominant outlook in American Protestantism well into the third quarter of the nineteenth century.[4]

Church history also shows that eschatology can be a major influence on the church's involvement in mission and social reform. The postmillennial hope provided much of the impulse for social improvement that characterized evangelical Protestantism in the earlier years of the nineteenth century. This combination of millennial hope and reforming zeal can be seen in Charles G. Finney, one of the preeminent evangelists of his age:

> Now the great business of the church is to reform the world—to put away every kind of sin. The Church of Christ was originally organized to be a body of reformers. . . . The Christian Church was designed to make aggressive movements in every direction—to lift up her voice and put forth her energies against iniquity in high and low places—to reform individuals, communities, and governments, and never rest until the Kingdom and the greatness of the Kingdom under the whole heaven shall be given to the people of the saints of the Most High God—until every form of iniquity shall be driven from the earth.[5]

---

4. Ibid., p. 48.
5. Cited in M. Darrol Bryant and Donald W. Dayton, eds., *The Coming Kingdom: Essays in American Millennialism and Eschatology* (Barrytown, N.Y.: International Religious Foundation, 1983), pp. 132–33.

Finney did not develop a fully articulated postmillennial
eschatology, but he did share in its general outlook and in
the sense of the dawning of the kingdom in history.

Strikingly different is the outlook of evangelist D. L.
Moody, who looked at the late-nineteenth-century world
in premillennial terms:

> I look on this world as a wrecked vessel. God has given me a
> lifeboat, and said to me, "Moody, save all you can." God will
> come in judgment and burn up this world . . . . This world
> is getting darker and darker; its rain is coming nearer and
> nearer; if you have any friends on this wreck unsaved you
> had better lose no time in getting them off . . . . Christ will
> save his Church, but he will save them finally by taking
> them out of the world.[6]

It seems clear that on such pessimistic premises, efforts by
Christians to improve the world are essentially a waste of
time and energy. The church's mission is to preach the
gospel, to gather the elect, to nurture the saints, and to
wait faithfully for Christ's return. Such conclusions were
drawn by many, though not all, American fundamen-
talists in the later nineteenth and earlier twentieth centuries.

The foregoing observations are not intended to imply
that eschatological positions are merely reflections of sociological conditions. They do, however, suggest that influences other than purely exegetical ones can affect the
church's outlook, and that these influences should be
taken into account in a self-critical way. Church history
also suggests that eschatological positions can significantly influence the church's understanding of the nature
and scope of its mission to the world. Awareness of these
trends in the history of biblical interpretation can assist
the contemporary reader of the Bible in his or her attempt
to allow the Scriptures, rather than worldly conditions, to

---

6. Ibid., pp. 133–34.

be the decisive influence in establishing an eschatological position.

The Conventional Wisdom: Bad-News Scenarios

"We are entering a period in which rapid population growth, the presence of obliterative weapons, and dwindling resources will bring international tensions to dangerous levels for an extended period," wrote Robert L. Heilbroner in *An Inquiry into the Human Prospect.*[7] Many observers today share Heilbroner's pessimistic outlook.

According to Robert S. McNamara, former president of the World Bank, without firm action to further reduce the population growth rate, world population will not stabilize below eleven billion. "At the national level," states McNamara, "rapid population growth translates into a steadily worsening employment future, massive city growth, pressure on food supplies, degradation of the environment, an increase in the number of the 'absolute poor,' and a stimulus to authoritarian government."[8]

The world population growth rate has dropped from 2 to 1.7 percent in recent years, but this means that world population will double in forty-one years instead of thirty-five.[9]

Much of this population increase will be concentrated in the already crowded cities of the Third World. By the year 2000, twenty out of twenty-five of the urban centers with more than ten million inhabitants are expected to be in

---

7. Robert L. Heilbroner, *An Inquiry into the Human Prospect* (New York: Norton, 1974), p. 127. For a recent pessimistic assessment of the American future, see Richard D. Lamm, *Megatraumas: America at the Year 2000* (Boston: Houghton Mifflin, 1985).

8. Robert S. McNamara, "Time Bomb or Myth: The Population Problem," *Foreign Affairs* 62:5 (1984): 1115.

9. "Warnings vs. Convention," *World Press Review*, October 1984, p. 37.

the Third World.[10] The population of these cities, now almost one billion people, will balloon to nearly four billion by 2025.[11]

The problems faced by Mexico City promise to be typical of the urban future. Its 17 million people could become 26 million or more by 2000, and killer smog, shocking lack of sanitation, and rampant corruption lower the quality of life for millions. In Calcutta, with a population of 10.2 million, 200,000 people depend upon begging for their sole source of income, and two thousand tons of garbage and trash litter the streets on a given day.[12]

Famine could be a recurring problem in the closing decades of the twentieth century, especially in Africa. Years of drought push the Sahara Desert southward, sometimes at the rate of ninety-three miles a year, taking over the once fertile land in its path. In Ethiopia, 200,000 people are believed to have died in the drought of 1973–74; in 1985, 6.4 million of the country's 34 million people were being affected.[13] During the mid-1980s, grain production per person in Africa was nearly one-fifth below the level of the late 1960s.[14]

The problem of resource depletion is said to be a grave one for the foreseeable future. According to the *Global 2000* report, during the 1990s world oil production will approach geological estimates of maximum production capacity, even with rapidly increasing petroleum prices. Regional water shortages could become more severe. Significant losses of world forests could occur as demand for

10. Sophie Bessis, "Tomorrow's World," *World Press Review*, October 1984, p. 40.

11. Robert W. Fox, "The Urban Explosion," *National Geographic*, August 1984, p. 179.

12. Otto Friedrich, "A Proud Capital's Distress," *Time*, August 6, 1984, pp. 26–27.

13. Michael Hanlon, "A Race Against Time," *World Press Review*, February 1985, pp. 37–38.

14. Lester R. Brown, *State of the World 1985* (New York: Norton, 1985), p. 21.

forest products and fuelwood increases. Serious deterioration of topsoil may occur worldwide due to erosion, des-
ertification, and waterlogging. Acid rain from increased
burning of fossil fuels threatens damage to lakes, soils,
and crops.[15]

The ultimate catastrophe, of course, is the danger of an
unlimited nuclear war between the superpowers. According to Jonathan Schell, "a full-scale nuclear holocaust
could lead to the extinction of mankind."[16] The grim vision of a burned-out planet where insects are the only
survivors is an apocalyptic scenario held by many today.

Teeming masses of humanity, widespread famine, resource depletion, nuclear holocaust: is it possible to be
hopeful for the future in the face of such predictions? Is
there also another side of the evidence to be considered?

Minority Opinion: Hopeful Scenarios

While many scientists and scholars today would appear
to share the somewhat pessimistic assessment of the
global future already sketched, there is a significant body
of scientific opinion that sees the world situation in quite
a different light. Julian L. Simon, Herman Kahn, and
their associates, for example, have directly challenged the
methodology, assumptions, use of facts, and conclusions of
the *Global 2000* report. "The facts, as I read them," states
Simon, "point in quite the opposite direction from the conclusions of *Global 2000* on every important aspect of their
prediction for which I could find any data."[17] The contributions to *The Resourceful Earth* show how in many instances the conclusions of *Global 2000* are based on faulty

15. *The Global 2000 Report,* vol. 1, pp. 2–3.

16. Jonathan Schell, *The Fate of the Earth* (New York: Knopf, 1982), p. 93.

17. Julian L. Simon, "Global Confusion 1980: A Hard Look at the Global
2000 Report," *Public Interest* no. 62 (Winter 1981): 3–20; for a fuller critique,
see Simon and Kahn, eds., *The Resourceful Earth,* a 565-page analysis of the
Global 2000 report.

or limited data, or on serious misinterpretations of the relevant data.

In several works Simon has challenged the widespread assumption that population growth inevitably retards economic development. According to Simon's studies of the available empirical data, even in the less developed nations additional children can induce people to work longer hours and invest more. Additional population can induce economies of scale and help support the development of better roads and communication systems. While in the short term—the first fifteen to twenty years of life—the new economic impact of an additional child is negative, in the long term the net effect upon per capita income comes to be positive, since the adult becomes a contributing member of society. The upshot of the matter is that even in the less-developed nations a moderate rate of population growth "is more likely to lead to a higher standard of living in the long run than either zero population growth or a high rate of population growth," argues Simon.[18] In the long term, when the whole sweep of recorded history is considered, the standard of living in the aggregate has risen along with the size of the world's population.[19] This is not to deny the existence of very real problems in the shorter term and in specific localities, but the long-term, global perspective must be kept in mind in order to achieve a balanced view of the issue.

With respect to world hunger and food production, there are some hopeful signs to be considered. New farm technologies in the past decade have had an important impact on global production averages. Genetically superior rice and wheat varieties developed by researchers in the Phil-

---

18. Julian L. Simon, *The Ultimate Resource* (Princeton: Princeton University Press, 1981), p. 286. See also Simon's earlier study, *The Economics of Population Growth* (Princeton: Princeton University Press, 1977), and "Resources, Population, Environment: An Oversupply of False Bad News," *Science* 208 (27 June 1980): 1431–37.

19. Simon, *The Ultimate Resource,* p. 345.

ippines and Mexico have more than tripled crops in some countries. In 1983 the world produced enough food to provide adequate diets for all its 4.7 billion people, problems of distribution and income notwithstanding.[20]

The United Nations Food and Agricultural Organization has stated that only half of the world's potential arable land is under cultivation today. As population growth rates reached a peak in the past two decades, world food production stayed well ahead everywhere except in Africa, where farming methods are least developed.[21]

In the longer term of human history food has tended to become cheaper with the passage of time, whether measured in terms of labor or relative prices. In the longer term more people lead to an increased market demand for food, which gives farmers incentives to grow more crops, and more research is done to increase productivity. Although hunger remains a very real problem, there are strong scientific reasons for believing that supplies of land and resources are in fact sufficient to provide adequate diets for the world's present and projected population.[22]

With respect to environmental pollution, some aspects of the problem, such as filth in city streets, purity of drinking water, and germs causing deadly contagious diseases, have lessened over the years. Other elements of the problem—gasoline fumes in the air, noise in the cities, atomic wastes—have become much more visible. In terms of the most inclusive measure of environmental quality—life expectancy—it is the case that in the United States and in the world as an aggregate life expectancy has increased significantly over the last century and may be expected to continue to increase.[23]

----

20. Ian Steele, "Winning the Battle," *World Press Review*, February 1985, p. 42.

21. Fred Pearce, "In Defense of Inaction," *World Press Review*, October 1984, p. 42.

22. Simon, *The Ultimate Resource*, pp. 68–69.

23. Ibid., pp. 142–43.

When measured in terms of the amount of human labor
and time required to purchase them, natural resources
and raw materials have become cheaper and less scarce
over time. An hour's work in the United States has bought
increasingly more wheat, copper, and oil, for example,
from 1800 to the present. The ability to recycle, to discover
substitutes, and to find ways to make existing resources
more productive implies that future generations can find
resources adequate to their needs. A single communi-
cations satellite in space, for example, provides intercon-
tinental telephone connections that otherwise would
require thousands of tons of copper.[24]

The specter of nuclear holocaust is indeed the most fear-
ful prospect on the contemporary scene. Those who believe
in the sovereign God of the Bible, however, have a basis for
living each day in hope rather than in a debilitating state
of anxiety and dread. Ultimately, it is *God* who is in control of world history and the fate of the earth, and not those
human rulers whose fingers are on the "nuclear button."
In the covenant with Noah God solemnly promised that he
would never again destroy all living creatures as he did in
the flood (Gen. 8:21–22). It is God's will that history continue until all nations have heard the gospel of the kingdom, and then the end will come (Matt. 24:14). Jesus
Christ will return not to a burned-out and lifeless planet,
but to one where people are complacently saying, "There is
peace and *security*" (1 Thess. 5:3, italics added). These
texts do not militate against responsible efforts to reduce
nuclear arms, nor do they preclude the possibility of a
limited nuclear exchange. They do, however, appear to
rule out the idea that God would permit a global, catastrophic nuclear holocaust prior to the return of Christ.[25]

24. Simon, "Resources, Population, Environment," p. 1435.

25. Some have suggested that the language of 2 Peter 3:10 suggests nuclear
weaponry ("the elements will be dissolved with fire"). This may in fact be
vivid, metaphorical language about divine judgment (cf. 2 Thess. 1:7, "when
the Lord Jesus is revealed from heaven with his mighty angels in flaming

Assessment and Conclusions

Which forecasters, the pessimists or the optimists, are more likely to be correct? Or could the actual outcome reflect a mixture of pessimistic and optimistic elements? In any case, are world conditions the decisive factor in determining one's eschatological outlook?

The position taken here is that world conditions per se have no decisive role in assessing eschatological positions, including the postmillennial option. The decisive factor in any determination should be biblical exegesis, not some attempt to read the "signs of the times." The postmillennial framework does not require or imply steadily improving world conditions from the present all the way to the beginning of the Great Revival. Temporal conditions are expected to be dramatically improved during the millennial era (cf. Isa. 2:2–4; 65:17–25), but the nature of world events prior to that time is an open question. It is important at this point not to confuse the postmillennial outlook with some secular notion of unbroken, continuous "progress" throughout history.

In the postmillennial framework the key to the church's hope is faith in the sovereignty of God and the power of the Spirit, not in world conditions as such. The growth of the mustard seed, the pervasive influence of the leaven (Matt. 13:31–33), the life-giving influence of the river flowing from the temple (Ezek. 47:1–12), and the dramatic growth of the stone from heaven (Dan. 2:34–35) are all the result of God's power and purpose, not worldly conditions or human effort. God's sovereign purpose will be realized, and even the "gates of Hades" will not be able to prevail against it.

Church history indeed indicates that the people of God frequently exhibit the greatest spiritual vitality when the

---

fire"). Even if it is to be taken literally, the final conflagration takes place at Christ's return, and not before. The people of God will be safe in Christ's presence.

external society is in a state of crisis or decline. The early
Christians displayed great spiritual vibrancy in the midst
of the political, social, economic, and moral turmoil of the
declining Roman Empire. Their faith and community life
was a powerful attraction to many uprooted people in the
midst of the confusion of that era. During the nineteenth
century, when the church was faced with the challenges of
urbanization, industrialization, higher criticism, Dar-
winism, and Marxism, the Protestant missionary enterprise was experiencing unprecedented expansion in
numbers and geographical reach. The church in China
since the late 1940s, with no foreign missionaries present
and under the domination of a Marxist regime, has experienced its greatest growth in history.

Human crisis can be an opportunity for the people of
God to experience and demonstrate the reality and power
of God's grace. Times of worldly crisis can show that the
heavenly treasure entrusted to the church indeed resides
in "earthen vessels," and that the transcendent power be-
longs to God, and not to any human institution (2 Cor. 4:7).

It is quite immaterial, then, to an assessment of the
postmillennial outlook whether world conditions improve
or decline in the short or intermediate term. Christ's kingdom will continue to expand, because the living, risen
Christ now is reigning victoriously at the Father's right
hand, subduing his foes (1 Cor. 15:25) and empowering the
church in its mission (Matt. 28:20). Whatever the immediate course of history might be, the believer's fundamental
outlook remains confident and hopeful, because the crucified One now lives and reigns forevermore, the King of
kings and Lord of lords (Rev. 19:16). "Hallelujah! For the
Lord our God the Almighty reigns" (Rev. 19:6).

8

Summary and Conclusions

It is now time to attempt to draw together the various lines of argument that have been presented and to consider some implications for the mission of the church and its ministry. The major themes of the preceding chapters may be briefly summarized as follows:

1. Postmillennialism is an eschatological outlook that anticipates a period of unprecedented revival in the church prior to the return of Christ, resulting from new outpourings of the Holy Spirit. This great revival is expected to be characterized by the church's numerical expansion and spiritual vitality. As a secondary result of the growing influence of Christian values, the world as a whole is expected to experience conditions of significant peace and economic improvement. This postmillennial expectation is not to be confused with notions of secular progress, faith in science and technology, a myth of inevitable progress, the social gospel, or "manifest destiny." The postmillennial outlook as here understood is grounded

fundamentally in Christology—in the vision of the victorious reign of the resurrected and ascended Lord at the right hand of the Father, who is actively extending the kingdom of God in the world through the power of his Word and Spirit. It is also noted that this general understanding of biblical eschatology was the dominant view among conservative Protestants for much of the nineteenth century. Its adherents have included such notable conservative theologians as John Owen, Jonathan Edwards, Charles Hodge, Robert L. Dabney, A. H. Strong, Benjamin B. Warfield, and others.

2. The expansive nature of God's redemptive purposes in the Old Testament is seen with particular clarity in the Abrahamic covenant and in the messianic promises and prophecies. In the Abrahamic covenant God reveals his purpose to ultimately bring spiritual blessings to all the families of the earth (Gen. 12:3). Abraham is challenged to believe that his spiritual descendants will be as numberless as the stars of heaven (Gen. 15:5–6) and as the sand on the seashore (Gen. 22:17). In subsequent Old Testament revelation it becomes clear that God's Messiah will be instrumental in bringing these universal blessings into history. Messianic psalms such as Psalms 2, 22, 72, and 110 depict a great king, God's Messiah, ruling over a vast kingdom that far transcends the boundaries of the nation Israel. This future messianic kingdom is also foreshadowed in the prophets. Isaiah 2:2–4 depicts a latter-day glory for the church, the spiritual Zion. Isaiah 9:6–7 speaks of the increasing reign of the new Davidic king—a prophecy whose fulfillment was initiated with the ascension of Christ to the right hand of the Father (Acts 2:30–31, 33–35). The peaceful conditions of the messianic reign in history are also spoken of in Isaiah 11:6–10 and 65:17–25. Ezekiel's vision of the miraculous life-giving river issuing from the temple, bringing new life and vitality to the desert (Ezek. 47:1–12), is understood to foreshadow the great outpouring of the Spirit that was

initiated at Pentecost (cf. John 7:37–39) but not terminated by that event. Daniel's vision of the mysterious stone from heaven that strikes the image and becomes a great mountain filling the whole earth (Dan. 2:31–35) is a picture of the victorious kingdom of Jesus Christ, overcoming all worldly opposition and spreading throughout the earth. Daniel's vision of the heavenly Son of man who is presented before the Ancient of Days (Dan. 7:13–14) depicts the reception of the ascended Christ by the Father in heaven and Christ's universal reign over the world from the right hand of God. These promises of the Abrahamic covenant and the messianic texts point forward in time to the New Testament's Great Commission (Matt. 28:19–20), where the church in its mission is the instrument through which the risen Christ in heaven progressively extends his lordship over the nations.

3. The examination of the New Testament data is organized along the following lines: first, texts pointing to the greatness of Christ the King; second, texts describing the growth of Christ's kingdom, and third, texts highlighting the final greatness of Christ's kingdom. Passages such as Matthew 28:18 and Ephesians 1:19–23 attest to the unlimited authority of the ascended Christ, a spiritual authority available to the church in its mission. The parables of growth (Matt. 12:31–33) show the dramatic growth of the kingdom from insignificant beginnings and its quiet but pervasive impact on the world. The spiritual weapons of the church's warfare have divine power to destroy strongholds (2 Cor. 10:3–5). Christ actively subdues his foes while reigning from the Father's right hand in heaven, a victorious process culminating in the overthrow of death itself at the parousia and final resurrection (1 Cor. 15:22–26). The final greatness of Christ's kingdom is foreshadowed in texts such as Revelation 7:9–10, where John speaks of a great multitude of the redeemed that no man can number. The apostle Paul looks forward to a time when the fullness of ethnic Israel will be saved (Rom.

11:25–26). The closing pages of the New Testament contain a magnificent picture of the New Jerusalem (Rev.
21:15–16), a vast city covering some 2,250,000 square
miles—a powerful image of the vastness of God's saving
purposes.

4. The course of church history and Christian missions
shows how the "mustard seed" has indeed demonstrated
remarkable growth over time. Against all human odds,
the Christian church won the Roman Empire. The history
of the expansion of the Christian church can be seen as a
series of nine major pulsations or epochs, five of which
were times of advance and four of which were times of
retreat. During the twentieth century Christianity became the most extensive and universal religion in history,
with organized Christian churches in every inhabited
country on earth. The Christian churches in Latin America, Africa, and Asia are growing dramatically. According
to church-growth expert C. Peter Wagner, "The last couple
of decades of the twentieth century hold forth more promise for the dynamic spread of the Christian faith around
the globe than any other period of time since Jesus turned
the water into wine."

5. Revelation 20:4–6 is examined first from premillennial and amillennial perspectives, and then from a
postmillennial standpoint. It is argued that the binding of
Satan (20:2) is a still future event. The phrase *thousand
years* is symbolic of a long period of spiritual prosperity for
the church. The "first resurrection" is taken to refer to the
future restoration and vindication of the cause for which
the martyrs died. This metaphorical understanding of the
"first resurrection" is supported by the striking correspon-
dence of the sequence of events described in Revelation
20:4–10. It is pointed out that even if Revelation 20:4–6 is
understood in a premillennial sense, there is no reason to
conclude that the Book of Revelation as a whole teaches a
pessimistic outlook for the church's prospects in history.
The risen Christ is Lord of lords and King of kings, and at

Summary and Conclusions

the end of history a great multitude of the redeemed that
no man can number will stand before the throne of God
(Rev. 7:9).

6. Texts which appear to be at variance with the
postmillennial outlook are examined. Passages indicating
the imminency of the parousia (e.g., 1 Cor. 7:29; James
5:9; 1 Peter 4:7; 1 John 2:18; Rev. 22:20) are understood
christologically and pneumatologically, rather than in a
merely chronological sense. In the death and resurrection
of Christ the events of the end time have already been
inaugurated, and through the presence of the Holy Spirit
the believing church experiences even now the reality and
power of Christ's victory that will in the future be visibly
manifested to the world. The "great tribulation" (Matt.
24:21) is taken to be the destruction of Jerusalem in A.D.
70 by the Roman armies of Titus. The church experiences
times of tribulation throughout history (John 16:33), but
tribulation does not imply defeat, for Christ has overcome
the world. Christ's sayings concerning the narrow door
and the narrow gate (Matt. 7:13–14; Luke 13:23–24) describe the limited response of the Jews to the earthly ministry of Jesus, and not the ultimate outcome of God's saving purpose, described elsewhere (as in the parables of
growth).

7. The impact of the church's perception of world conditions on its eschatological expectation is examined. It is
noted that pessimistic conditions tend to favor the spread
of premillennial understandings, whereas more hopeful
world conditions have promoted the postmillennial outlook. Pessimistic and optimistic projections for the coming
decades are examined. It is argued that the case for
postmillennialism must be assessed on the grounds of biblical exegesis and not on the basis of secular assessments
of the world condition. The postmillennial outlook does
not involve a scenario of uninterrupted worldly progress
in the interval between the present and the beginning of
the great revival. This period of great spiritual vitality

and growth for the church is not dependent on world conditions, but solely on the sovereign authority of the risen Christ and the power of the Holy Spirit.

This reexamination of the postmillennial tradition has centered not on chronological speculations, date-setting, or readings of the "signs of the times," but rather on the biblical vision of the victorious kingdom of the resurrected and ascended Christ. Eschatology is seen to be fundamentally an outworking of Christology, and not a projected calendar of the future events. Given the biblical witness to the victory and present reign of Jesus Christ, the church can look to the future with realism and hope. The expansion of Christ's kingdom in history is marked by opposition, conflict, persecution, and temporary setbacks and defeats. The overall trend of history is clear, however. The mighty stone from heaven will overcome all worldly opposition and grow to fill the entire earth. This biblical vision can give today's church a tremendous impetus for its missionary and social task, as indeed it did to earlier generations of Christians. Today's church needs to turn its attention away from any preoccupations with worldly conditions in order to grasp anew, by faith, the magnificent vision of the mighty Christ at the Father's right hand who is Lord of lords and King of kings. Christ the mighty King reigns *now,* and his invincible power is available to the church. It is in this hope that Christ's disciples can labor confidently and perseveringly for the extension of his kingdom in the world. "Hallelujah! For the Lord our God the Almighty reigns" (Rev. 19:6).

Bibliography

Books

Angus, S. *The Environment of Early Christianity*. London: Duckworth, 1914.

Archer, Gleason L., Jr., trans. *Jerome's Commentary on Daniel*. Grand Rapids: Baker, 1958.

Barclay, William. *The Revelation of John*. 2 vols. Philadelphia: Westminster, 1976.

Bark, William Carroll. *Origins of the Medieval World*. Stanford: Stanford University Press, 1958.

Barney, Gerald O. *The Global 2000 Report to the President*. 3 vols. Washington, D.C.: U.S. Government Printing Office, 1980.

Barrett, C. K. *A Commentary on the First Epistle to the Corinthians*. New York: Harper and Row, 1968.

Barrett, David B., ed. *World Christian Encyclopedia*. Nairobi: Oxford University Press, 1982.

135

Barth, Markus. *The Broken Wall: A Study of the Epistle to the Ephesians*. Chicago: Judson, 1959.

Beasley-Murray, G. R. *The Book of Revelation*. Grand Rapids: Eerdmans, 1974.

Blackman, Philip, trans. *Mishnayoth*. 7 vols. New York: Judaica Press, 1963.

Boettner, Loraine, *The Millennium*. Philadelphia: Presbyterian and Reformed, 1957.

Boutflower, Charles. *In and Around the Book of Daniel*. Grand Rapids: Zondervan, 1963.

Bratcher, Robert G. *A Translator's Guide to the Gospel of Mark*. London: United Bible Societies, 1981.

Broadus, John A. *Commentary on the Gospel of Matthew*. Philadelphia: American Baptist Publication Society, 1886.

Brown, Lester R. *State of the World 1985*. New York: Norton, 1985.

Brown, Raymond E. *The Epistles of John*. Garden City, N.Y.: Doubleday, 1982.

_____. *The Gospel According to John*. Garden City, N.Y.: Doubleday, 1966.

Bruce, F. F. *The Epistle of Paul to the Romans*. Grand Rapids: Eerdmans, 1963.

Bryant, M. Darrol, and Donald W. Dayton, eds. *The Coming Kingdom: Essays in American Millennialism and Eschatology*. Barrytown, N.Y.: International Religious Foundation, 1983.

Calvin, John. *Commentaries on the First Book of Moses, Called Genesis*. Translated by John King. 2 vols. Grand Rapids: Eerdmans, 1948.

_____. *Commentary on the Book of the Prophet Isaiah*. Translated by William Pringle. 4 vols. Grand Rapids: Eerdmans, 1948.

_____. *Institutes of the Christian Religion*. Edited by John T. McNeill. Translated by Ford Lewis Battles. 2 vols. Philadelphia: Westminster, 1960.

_____. *The Second Epistle of Paul the Apostle to the Corinthians and the Epistles to Timothy, Titus, and Philemon*. Edited by David W. Torrance and Thomas F. Torrance. Translated by T. A. Smail. Grand Rapids: Eerdmans, 1964.

Cassuto, Umberto. *A Commentary on the Book of Genesis*. Translated by Israel Abrahams. 2 vols. Jerusalem: Magnes Press, 1964.

Childs, Brevard S. *The New Testament as Canon: An Introduction.* Philadelphia: Fortress, 1984.

Chilton, David. *Paradise Restored.* Tyler, Tex.: American Bureau for Economic Research, 1984.

Clouse, Robert G., ed. *The Meaning of the Millennium: Four Views.* Downers Grove: InterVarsity, 1977.

Conzelmann, Hans. *1 Corinthians: A Commentary on the First Epistle to the Corinthians.* Edited by George W. MacRae. Translated by James W. Leitch. Philadelphia: Fortress, 1975.

Dabney, Robert L. *Lectures in Systematic Theology.* 1878. Grand Rapids: Zondervan, 1972.

Davies, W. D. *Paul and Rabbinic Judaism.* London: S.P.C.K., 1955.

Dibelius, Martin, and Hans Conzelmann. *The Pastoral Epistles: A Commentary on the Pastoral Epistles.* Edited by Helmut Koester. Translated by Philip Buttolph and Adela Yarbro. Philadelphia: Fortress, 1972.

Dodds, E. R. *Pagan and Christian in an Age of Anxiety: Some Aspects of Religious Experience from Marcus Aurelius to Constantine.* Cambridge: Cambridge University Press, 1965.

Easton, Burton Scott. *The Pastoral Epistles.* London: SCM, 1948.

Edwards, Jonathan. *Apocalyptic Writings.* Vol. 5 of *The Works of Jonathan Edwards.* Edited by Stephen J. Stein. New Haven: Yale University Press, 1977.

Erickson, Millard J. *Contemporary Options in Eschatology: A Study of the Millennium.* Grand Rapids: Baker, 1977.

Fairbairn, Patrick. *The Interpretation of Prophecy.* 1856. London: Banner of Truth, 1964.

Fonck, Leopold. *The Parables of the Gospel: An Exegetical and Practical Explanation.* New York: Frederick Pustet Co., 1914.

Foulkes, Francis. *The Epistle of Paul to the Ephesians: An Introduction and Commentary.* Grands Rapids: Eerdmans, 1963.

Geldenhuys, Norval. *Commentary on the Gospel of Luke.* Grand Rapids: Eerdmans, 1981.

Godet, Frederic. *A Commentary on the Gospel of St. Luke.* 5th ed. Translated by M. D. Cusin. 2 vols. Reprint ed. Edinburgh: T. and T. Clark, 1976.

Goodwin, Thomas. *An Exposition of Ephesians.* Reprint ed. Evansville, Ind.: Sovereign Grace Book Club, 1958.

Green, Michael. *Evangelism in the Early Church*. London: Hodder and Stoughton, 1970.

Hammer, Raymond. *The Book of Daniel*. Cambridge: Cambridge University Press, 1976.

Hay, David M. *Glory at the Right Hand: Psalm 110 in Early Christianity*. Nashville: Abingdon, 1973.

Heilbroner, Robert L. *An Inquiry into the Human Prospect*. New York: Norton, 1974.

Hendriksen, William. *More than Conquerors*. Grand Rapids: Baker, 1939.

Henry, Matthew. *Commentary on the Whole Bible*. Edited by Leslie F. Church. 1-vol. ed. Reprint ed. Grand Rapids: Zondervan, 1961.

Hering, Jean. *The First Epistle of Saint Paul to the Corinthians*. London: Epworth, 1962.

Hodge, Charles. *An Exposition of the Second Epistle to the Corinthians*. 1859. Grand Rapids: Baker, 1980.

_____. *Systematic Theology*. 3 vols. 1872–73. Grand Rapids: Eerdmans, 1968.

Kalt, Edmund, ed. *Herder's Commentary on the Psalms*. Translated by Bernard Fritz. Westminster, Md.: Newman Press, 1961.

Keil, K. F., and Franz Delitzsch. *Biblical Commentary on the Old Testament*. Translated by James Martin. 25 vols. *The Pentateuch*, 3 vols.; *The Psalms*, 3 vols.; *The Twelve Minor Prophets*, 2 vols. Grand Rapids: Eerdmans, 1949.

Kik, J. Marcellus. *An Eschatology of Victory*. Nutley, N.J.: Presbyterian and Reformed, 1971.

Kimball, William. *The Great Tribulation*. 1983. Grand Rapids: Baker, 1984.

Lacocque, Andre. *The Book of Daniel*. Translated by David Pellauer. Atlanta: John Knox, 1978.

Ladd, George E. *A Commentary on the Revelation of John*. Grand Rapids: Eerdmans, 1972.

Lamm, Richard D. *Megatraumas: America at the Year 2000*. Boston: Houghton Mifflin, 1985.

Latourette, Kenneth Scott. *The Christian Outlook*. New York: Harper and Row, 1948.

_____. *The First Five Centuries*. Vol. 1 of *History of the Expansion of Christianity*. New York: Harper and Row, 1937.

_____. *A History of Christianity*. London: Eyre and Spottiswoode, n.d.

Leenhardt, Franz J. *The Epistle to the Romans: A Commentary*. Translated by Harold Knight. Cleveland: World, 1961.

Lenski, R. C. H. *The Interpretation of St. John's Revelation*. Minneapolis: Augsburg, 1961.

_____. *The Interpretation of St. Luke's Gospel*. Columbus, Ohio: Wartburg, 1946.

_____. *The Interpretation of St. Matthew's Gospel*. Columbus, Ohio: Wartburg, 1943.

_____. *The Interpretation of St. Paul's Epistle to the Romans*. Minneapolis: Augsburg, 1961.

_____. *The Interpretation of St. Paul's First and Second Epistles to the Corinthians*. Minneapolis: Augsburg, 1961.

Lightfoot, J. B. *Saint Paul's Epistles to the Colossians and to Philemon*. London: Macmillan, 1882.

MacMullen, Ramsay. *Christianizing the Roman Empire: A.D. 100–400*. New Haven: Yale University Press, 1984.

Marshall, I. Howard. *The Epistles of John*. Grand Rapids: Eerdmans, 1978.

Momigliano, Arnoldo, ed. *The Conflict Between Paganism and Christianity in the Fourth Century*. London: Oxford University Press, 1963.

Moore, A. L. *The Parousia in the New Testament*. Leiden: E. J. Brill, 1966.

Morris, Leon. *The First and Second Epistles to the Thessalonians*. Grand Rapids: Eerdmans, 1959.

_____. *The Revelation of St. John: An Introduction and Commentary*. Grand Rapids: Eerdmans, 1969.

Mounce, Robert H. *The Book of Revelation*. Grand Rapids: Eerdmans, 1977.

Mowinckel, Sigmund. *He That Cometh: The Messiah Concept in the Old Testament and Later Judaism*. Translated by G. W. Anderson. New York: Abingdon, 1956.

Owen, John. *The Works of John Owen*. Edited by William H. Goold. 16 vols. 1850. London: Banner of Truth, 1967.

Perowne, J. J. Stewart. *The Book of Psalms*. 2 vols. Andover: Warren F. Draper, 1894.

Rad, Gerhard von. *Genesis: A Commentary*. Translated by John H. Marks. Philadelphia: Westminster, 1961.

Russell, J. Stuart. *The Parousia: A Study of the New Testament Doctrine of Our Lord's Second Coming*. Reprint ed. Grand Rapids: Baker, 1983.

Schaff, Philip, ed. *The Creeds of Christendom*. 6th ed. 3 vols. Reprint ed. Grand Rapids: Baker, 1983.

Schell, Jonathan. *The Fate of the Earth*. New York: Knopf, 1982.

Simon, Julian L. *The Economics of Population Growth*. Princeton: Princeton University Press, 1977.

_____. *The Ultimate Resource*. Princeton: Princeton University Press, 1981.

Simon, Julian L., and Herman Kahn, eds. *The Resourceful Earth: A Response to Global 2000*. New York: Blackwell, 1984.

Smith, Timothy L. *Revivalism and Social Reform in Mid-Nineteenth-Century America*. Nashville: Abingdon, 1957.

Strong, A. H. *Systematic Theology*. Philadelphia: Judson, 1907.

Swete, Henry Barclay. *Commentary on the Apocalypse of St. John*. Grand Rapids: Eerdmans, 1951.

Toon, Peter, ed. *Puritans, the Millennium and the Future of Israel: Puritan Eschatology 1600 to 1660*. Cambridge: James Clark, 1970.

Trench, Richard C. *Notes on the Parables of Our Lord*. New York: N. Tibbals and Sons, 1879.

Wagner, C. Peter. *On the Crest of the Wave: Becoming a World Christian*. Ventura, Calif.: Regal, 1983.

Walvoord, John F. *The Revelation of Jesus Christ: A Commentary*. Chicago: Moody, 1966.

Warfield, Benjamin Breckinridge. *Biblical and Theological Studies*. Edited by Samuel G. Craig. Philadelphia: Presbyterian and Reformed, 1952.

Young, Edward J. *The Book of Isaiah*. 3 vols. Grand Rapids: Eerdmans, 1965.

Zimmerli, Walther. *Ezekiel 2*. Philadelphia: Fortress, 1983.

Articles

Aguirre, Rafael. "Early Christian House Churches." *Theology Digest* 32:2 (1985): 152.

Bahnsen, Greg. "The Prima Facie Acceptability of Postmillennialism." *Journal of Christian Reconstruction* 3:2 (1976–77):48–105.

Barclay, William. "Matthew 24." *Expository Times* 70 (1959): 326–30.

Bauckham, Richard J. "The Delay of the Parousia." *Tyndale Bulletin* 31 (1980): 3–36.

Beasley-Murray, G. R. "The Interpretation of Daniel 7." *Catholic Biblical Quarterly* 45:1 (1983): 44–58.

Beckwith, Clarence Augustine. "The Millennium." *The New Schaff-Herzog Encyclopedia of Religious Knowledge,* edited by Samuel Macauley Jackson. Vol. 7. New York: Funk and Wagnalls, 1910.

Bessis, Sophie. "Tomorrow's World." *World Press Review,* October 1984, p. 40.

Bietenhard, Hans. "The Millennial Hope in the Early Church." *Scottish Journal of Theology* 6 (1953): 12–30.

Chao, Jonathan. "The Structure of House Churches." *China and the Church Today,* March-April 1983, p. 8.

Clouse, Robert G. "Millennium, Views of the." *Evangelical Dictionary of Theology,* edited by Walter A. Elwell. Grand Rapids: Baker, 1984.

Coote, Robert T. "The Uneven Growth of Conservative Evangelical Missions." *International Bulletin of Missionary Research* 6:3 (1982): 118–23.

Davies, J. G. "The Genesis of Belief in an Imminent Parousia." *Journal of Theological Studies* n.s. 14 (1963): 104–7.

Deere, Jack S. "Premillennialism in Rev. 20:4–6." *Bibliotheca Sacra* 135 (1978): 58–73.

Di Lella, Alexander A. "The One in Human Likeness and the Holy Ones of the Most High in Daniel 7." *Catholic Biblical Quarterly* 39:1 (1977): 1–19.

Fox, Robert W. "The Urban Explosion." *National Geographic,* August 1984, p. 179.

Friedrich, Otto. "A Proud Capital's Distress." *Time,* August 6, 1984, pp. 26–27.

Granata, G. "La 'sinapis' del Vangelo." *Bibliotheca Orientalis* 24 (1982): 175–77.

Grigsby, Bruce. "Gematria and John 21:11: Another Look at Ezekiel 47:10." *Expository Times* 95:6 (1984): 177–78.

Gundry, Stanley N. "Hermeneutics or *Zeitgeist* as the Determining

Factor in the History of Eschatologies?" *Journal of the Evangelical Theological Society* 20:1 (1977): 45–55.

Hanlon, Michael. "A Race Against Time." *World Press Review,* February 1985, pp. 37–38.

Hiers, Richard H. "The Delay of the Parousia in Luke-Acts." *New Testament Studies* 20 (1974): 145–55.

Horne, Charles M. "The Meaning of the Phrase, 'And Thus All Israel Will Be Saved' (Rom. 11:26)." *Evangelical Theological Society Journal* 21 (1978): 329–34.

Hughes, J. A. "Revelation 20:4–6 and the Question of the Millennium." *Westminster Theological Journal* 35 (1973): 281–302.

Kline, M. G. "The First Resurrection." *Westminster Theological Journal* 37 (1975): 366–75.

Lambrecht, J. "Paul's Christological Use of Scripture in 1 Cor. 15:20–28." *New Testament Studies* 28 (1982): 502–27.

Loader, W. R. G. "Christ at the Right Hand—Ps. 110:1 in the New Testament." *New Testament Studies* 24 (1978): 199–217.

Longenecker, Richard N. "The Nature of Paul's Early Eschatology." *New Testament Studies* 31 (1985): 85–95.

McArthur, Harvey K. "The Parable of the Mustard Seed." *Catholic Biblical Quarterly* 33 (1971): 198–210.

McNamara, Robert S. "Time Bomb or Myth: The Population Problem." *Foreign Affairs* 62:5 (1984): 1107–31.

MacRae, George W. "The Meaning and Evolution of the Feast of Tabernacles." *Catholic Biblical Quarterly* 22 (1960): 251–76.

Michaels, J. R. "The First Resurrection: A Response." *Westminster Theological Journal* 39 (1976): 100–109.

Minear, Paul S. "The Cosmology of the Apocalypse." In *Current Issues in New Testament Interpretation: Essays in Honor of Otto A. Piper,* edited by William Klassen and Graydon F. Snyder. New York: Harper and Brothers, 1962.

Moorhead, James H. "The Erosion of Postmillennialism in American Religious Thought, 1865–1925." *Church History* 53:1 (1984): 61–77.

Owen, H. P. "The Parousia of Christ in the Synoptic Gospels." *Scottish Journal of Theology* 12 (1959): 171–92.

Pace, G. "La senepa del Vangelo." *Bibliotheca Orientalis* 22 (1980): 119–23.

Page, Sydney H. T. "Revelation 20 and Pauline Eschatology." *Journal of the Evangelical Theological Society* 23:1 (1980): 31–43.

Pearce, Fred. "In Defense of Inaction." *World Press Review,* October 1984, p. 42.

Quandt, Jean B. "Religion and Social Thought: The Secularization of Postmillennialism." *American Quarterly* 25 (1973): 390–409.

Shepherd, N. "The Resurrections of Revelation 20." *Westminster Theological Journal* 37 (1974): 34–43.

Simon, Julian L. "Global Confusion 1980: A Hard Look at the Global 2000 Report." *Public Interest* no. 62 (Winter 1981): 3–20.

——————. "Resources, Population, Environment: An Oversupply of False Bad News." *Science* 208 (27 June 1980): 1431–37.

Smith, Timothy L. "Righteousness and Hope: Christian Holiness and the Millennial Vision in America, 1800–1900." *American Quarterly* 31:1 (1979): 21–45.

Sproule, J. A. "The Problem of the Mustard Seed." *Grace Theological Journal* 1 (1980): 37–42.

Steele, Ian. "Winning the Battle." *World Press Review,* February 1985, p. 42.

Summers, Ray. "Matthew 24–25: An Exposition." *Review and Expositor* 59 (1962): 501–11.

Talbert, Charles H. "II Peter and the Delay of the Parousia." *Vigilae Christianae* 20 (1966): 137–45.

Torbet, Robert J. "Expansion of Christianity (Ancient)." *Twentieth Century Encyclopedia of Religious Knowledge,* edited by Lefferts A. Loetscher. Grand Rapids: Baker, 1955.

Wagner, C. Peter. "The Greatest Church Growth Is Beyond Our Shores." *Christianity Today* 28:8 (1984): 25.

Wallis, W. B. "The Problem of an Intermediate Kingdom in 1 Corinthians 15:20–28." *Evangelical Theological Society Journal* 18 (1975): 229–42.

Scripture Index

Printed in the United States
89154LV00001B/70-81/A